After the Lovedeath

After the Lovedeath

Sexual Violence and the Making of Culture

Lawrence Kramer

UNIVERSITY OF CALIFORNIA PRESS

Berkeley   Los Angeles   London

Portions of three sections of this book are adapted from my
article "Victorian Poetry/Oedipal Politics," *Victorian Poetry*
29 (1991): 351–64.

University of California Press
Berkeley and Los Angeles, California

University of California Press, Ltd.
London, England

Library of Congress Cataloging-in-Publication Data

Kramer, Lawrence, 1946–
    After the lovedeath : sexual violence and the making of
culture / Lawrence Kramer.
        p.   cm.
    Includes bibliographic references and index
    ISBN 0-520-21012-3 (cloth : alk. paper)
        1. Sex role.   2. Sex crimes—psychological aspects.
3. Women—Crimes against—Psychological aspects.
4. Masculinity (Psychology)   5. Femininity (Psychology)
6. Sex role in art.   7. Violence in art.   8. Sex in art.
9. Sex in music.   I. Title.   II. Title: After the lovedeath.
    HQ1075.K73   1997
    305.3—dc21   97-4933

Printed in the United States of America
9 8 7 6 5 4 3 2 1

The paper used in this publication meets the minimum
requirements of American National Standards for
Information Sciences—Permanence of Paper for Printed
Library Materials, ANSI Z39.48-1984.

Contents

Acknowledgments / ix

*After the Lovedeath: Sexual Violence
and the Making of Culture* / 1

Oedipus Tyrannos (Swellfoot the Tyrant) / 21

A Little Extra Piece / 26

"Any man has to, wants to, needs to" / 30

The Bathers / 34

Brimstone / 37

A Whole Piece More / 38

Violence and Misrecognition / 41

(Coup de) Grace Notes / 44

A Portmanteau / 46

The First Wolf Dream (1951) / 47

Reorientations / 50

Aria / 55

Gensynderergy / 60

Le Baton ivre / 61

Lifelines / 65

Fascinatin' Rhythm / 77

Mincing Along / 81

Unedited Text of the Second Wolf Dream (ca. 1972) / 85

A Blind Spot / 87

Love Knots / 90

The Pobble That Has No Toes / 95

Becoming Disowned / 97

The Politest Castration / 99

A Sight for Sore Eyes / 101

"In the far south" / 105

Aural Sex / 108

Counterparts / 113

Obsequies / 114

Just Married / 116

Inside Stories / 119

Arietta / 123

The Pozdnyshevian Art / 125

Diva / 129

An Asymmetry / 132

"Isolde sinks, as if transfigured . . ." / 134

"Softly in Brangäne's arms . . ." / 136

"Onto Tristan's body" / *139*

Chop Logic / *141*

Tall Tales / *146*

Cogito E_go Sum / *147*

Cavatina / *148*

Pleiades / *152*

Clef Change / *153*

Epiphany / *155*

Conundrum / *158*

Minstrels / *159*

Tableau vivant / *161*

Passing / *164*

Riddles of the Sphinx / *169*

Straight and Narrow / *170*

Tuning up: The "Kreutzer" Sonata / *171*

The Soundtrack of the Sirens: Prague to Hollywood / *173*

Ruling Bodies / *177*

Bad Signs / *180*

In My Second / *184*

Heterosexless Desire / *185*

"I Wanna Be a Football Hero" / *189*

Aubade / *191*

Ah! But / *193*

Cyanosis / *194*

Homoerogenous Zones / *197*

"It glides quickly in through my ears" / 201

Latent Remedies / 203

The Law Is an Ass / 206

Ménages à Trois / 208

Ralph and Alice / 210

Ear to the Ground / 213

Tinnitus / 215

Pole Star / 224

The Closet within the Closet / 226

Conquest of the Pole / 229

Breaking Ranks / 231

Odd Couples / 234

Depolarizing / 236

"Impassioned to the point of obscenity" / 238

Erotoautism / 243

Differences / 247

Piece Work / 249

Holding It In / 259

At the Crossroads / 261

The White Wolf / 264

Notes / 265

Bibliography / 269

Index / 277

Acknowledgments

I have been especially fortunate in the advice and encouragement offered to me about this book. My thanks go to Doris Kretschmer, my editor for a fourth time at the University of California Press, whose guidance, as usual, has been invaluable; to Erika Büky and Carolyn Hill for expert project supervision and copyediting; to Richard Leppert, for stimulating exchanges on "The Kreutzer Sonata" that helped spark the project; to Susan McClary, for wise suggestions and for making it possible, in the first place, to talk about music and gender seriously in the same breath; to Sandy Petrey, for a generous reading that taught me some things about my own text; and to Ruth Solie, for her own wise suggestions and for sharing her unsurpassed savvy about the world of gender studies. Above all, however, I would like to thank Nancy Leonard, whose understanding of gender issues has so informed mine over the years that she can claim to be a collaborator in this book—at least in the good parts.

After the Lovedeath

Sexual Violence and the Making of Culture

I knew a man once did a girl in
Any man might do a girl in
Any man has to, needs to, wants to
Once in a lifetime, do a girl in.
                    T. S. Eliot, Sweeney Agonistes

This book proposes that the forms of selfhood mandated as normal in modern Western culture both promote and rationalize violence against women. Even if unacted, the possibility of sexual violence ripples in the air like rising heat, visible and invisible at the same time. Far from being haunted or threatened by this possibility, normal selfhood is permeated by it. Both men and women alike are enjoined to construct heterosexual gender identities based on a mercurial love-hate relationship to whatever is understood as femininity. Violence simply transcribes this attitude as action. Virtually everyone regrets it, including those who inflict it. Yet it persists, indifferent to social distinctions and impervious to sociologically inspired remedies—sensitivity training, better role models, more ideal media images—that try to promote less tolerance in women and less aggressiveness in men. The tendency to sexual violence seems lodged in the very core of ordinary subjectivity like a bone in the throat.

This predicament arises, not from any particular definition of what it means to be feminine or masculine, but from the way femininity and masculinity are distinguished. The two genders may be constructed, performed, and lived in any number of ways, as long as femininity constitutes the radically ambivalent polar opposite of a radically unambivalent masculinity. The conflicts and confusions that inevitably result when people prove unwilling or unable to fulfill this rigid mandate play themselves out roughly on women's bodies, both real and imaginary. Zealots of the system, men transfixed by some masculine ideal, feel called upon to punish the less zealous. Sometimes their rod falls on the "unmanly" men who embrace ambivalence, but the primary objects of punishment are the women whose paradigmatic role it is to embody ambivalence. A woman may be judged to deserve punishment whenever she steps beyond her paradigmatic position; her role as an embodiment is protected from injury by doing injury to her body. A woman may come to deserve such punishment either by affirming whatever features of femininity are stigmatized in her particular milieu or by unmasking the condition of stigma-free masculinity there as an illusion. Sometimes, however, she may seem to do one of these things merely by being alive.

Does each man kill the thing he loves, as Oscar Wilde maintains? If so, it is because the thing he loves can be embodied only in the thing he hates. The woman he desires (so he is told) is the bearer of a femininity that he is required to devalue. Yet her femininity (so he is told) is precisely what enables him to desire her. He can love her only insofar as there is something in her he cannot love. It does not matter whether his feelings are crude or refined, earthy or idealized, passionate or companionable. What is loved and what is hated are necessarily interwoven into the texture of the same person's being. And the person—the woman—pays.

After the Lovedeath suggests why and how this is so and imagines alternatives. In form, alternative in itself, the book is a mosaic: a piecing together of reflections formal and informal, longer and shorter, on the interplay between sexual violence and the complex ways in which we imagine ourselves as gendered beings. The sources of reflection are passages drawn from a variety of imaginative media, including fiction, opera, poetry, instrumental music, visual imagery, even dreams. The aim of reflection is to reach a better understanding of the cultural situation by interpreting it in the light of these works of imagination. In a reversal of familiar procedures, culture takes on the role of a text to be read in the context of representation, expressivity, and fantasy. Such imaginative processes can neither be translated directly into "real" life, as a certain repressive moralism fears, nor be entirely disengaged from it, as a certain repressive aestheticism wishes. In one of their many dimensions, they form treasuries of suggestion, nurseries of attitude, that can help produce, sustain, and foster insight into complex cultural realities. When we listen to music or hear the music of language, we resonate with such realities; when we gaze with strained attention at imaginary scenes on the stage or screen, including the screen of the mind's eye when we read or dream, we are engaged in the making of culture, our making by culture, which includes the mechanism both of sexual violence and, someday perhaps, of its undoing.

⤎∞⤏

I begin with Franz Schubert because he once wrote music for a dream of mine. I was in a thick wood where wild animals, wolves or bears, might be lurking, but I took so much pleasure in observing the flowers—some of my favorite flowers were there, especially the pinkish-yellow roses—that I was careless of danger. The dream also had a soundtrack, a "melting" melody, endlessly repeated, that I later recognized (or believed) to be by Schubert, a theme he used in the ballet music to the drama *Rosamunde* and used again in one of his Impromptus for piano. The whole scene was suffused with a distinct sense of sexual pleasure.

I return to this dream later, but to begin with I want to note only its most obvious element. The dream finds pleasure in a dangerous place, a sexual pleasure and a place linked with Schubert. What was the place? And what was the danger?

One clue comes from another composer, Robert Schumann, who admired Schubert and was perhaps unsettled by Schubert's early nineteenth-century reputation as a kind of musical idiot savant: a childlike figure, clumsy, bashful, awkward in speech and writing, lacking in self-possession, and yet a genius from whom, somehow, exquisite music flowed. Perhaps *too* exquisite: for there was felt to be something wrong with this music. For all its beauty, it lacked virility, at least in comparison with the masculine ideal embodied, inevitably, by Beethoven. Schumann sets out to rescue Schubert from this invidious comparison, though only at the cost of assenting to it. In relation to Beethoven, Schumann wrote,

Schubert was indeed a feminine composer, but in relation to all other composers he was masculine enough. Beethoven, in this reading, is a violent figure, or a figure—a personification—of violence: one who feminizes others but who can never himself be feminized. "The man [Beethoven]," writes Schumann, "commands;" the woman [Schubert] "pleads" (117). In this hypervirile role, Beethoven stands as the embodiment of musical culture itself: stern, unyielding, commanding, his name the name of the musical Father. Before this Beethoven, Schubert is yielding, dependent, permeable. Yet this same Schubert can himself lay claim to the name of the father if only one can forget (but one can never forget) the figure of Beethoven behind him.

This tale of the gender of musical genius gives, in allegory, the gist of this book. Bluntly stated, my argument is that in our gender identities, all of us—men and women alike—are Schuberts, none of us a Beethoven. Between the sixteenth and the eighteenth centuries, the position in which Schumann recognized Schubert became the normative position of the subject in Western culture, and so it remains today. For both men and women, to become a subject, to acquire an identity, is to assume a position of femininity in relation to a masculinity that always belongs to someone else. This other is the wielder and bearer of authority in all its forms, social, moral, and cultural; both pleasure and truth are in his charge; yet no man, and certainly no woman, can securely identify with this masculine subject-position. Instead, biological men are directed to occupy a position that is simultaneously masculine in relation to a visible, public, feminine position, and feminine in relation to an unstated, often unconscious position held by the figure (trope, image, or person) of another man. The same men are directed to repress their knowledge that this doubling of polarity by the dim, ever-looming figure of the other man renders their own position masculine in content but feminine in structure. Every man who commands is secretly a woman who pleads—and blissfully obeys—but who struggles not to know it.

The reward for maintaining this repression is the fiction of unambivalent self-possession: the fiction of holding the absolutely masculine subject-position that in truth no one can hold. In the language of Jacques Lacan, it is the fiction of having the phallus (note that there is only one). To be sure, this fiction is unstable, sometimes even ridiculous. But in social terms it translates—for some men—into the privileges of a practical, manifest, functional masculinity.

For some men. Not everyone with a penis is entitled to even a fictitiously absolute masculinity; the masculinity of some must wear its contingency visibly. Racial, sexual, and social polarities cut across gender polarity in complex ways and further deplete the position of entitlement. Black men, for example, still do not have the unquestioned right to claim masculine privilege in relation to white women, and they may find that this racial limitation undercuts their ability to claim the socially inferior version of that privilege available through black women. In many cases, the darker the man, the greater the difficulty. Gay men, or men suspected of being gay, are likely to find themselves assigned to a feminine position regardless of whether their behavior is effeminate and regardless of whether they are met with open homophobia. They may also contend for privilege among themselves by stigmatizing effeminacy; *fag* or *fairy* functions as an insult among gay men the way *nigger* does among black men. These sorts of baroque convolution in social logic are easy to take as farcical in the telling; in the living they are simply hard to take. To acknowledge such complexities is important at this point, because I am forced mostly to ignore them in pursuing the more than ample complexities of gender considered in isolation.

Like all defense mechanisms, the repression of the knowledge that all subjective positionality is structurally "feminine" works only sporadically. Masculine identity is always shadowed by disavowed reminders that it is borrowed, simulated, relative—more a costume than an essence. Meanwhile, and partly in consequence, biological women are made to bear the main burden of occupying the official, visible feminine position, and in so doing of maintaining the fiction that the position held by men is genuinely polarized, absolutely masculine in both content and structure.

This symbolic function operates in a multitude of contexts, social, erotic, aesthetic, narrative, and ideological. It underwrites both the empirical subordination of women and the ideological ruses by which men and women alike come to legitimate that subordination, often while vigorously denying that they do so. Also underwritten is the hair-trigger anxiety about gender boundaries that no man can fully escape, that so often symbolizes itself as the threat of castration or liquefaction, and that manifests itself reactively as misogyny and sexual violence. For the basis of the cultural authority associated with the impossible position of absolute masculinity is precisely the threat of violence.

This violence is paradoxical by nature and thrives, alas, on the paradox. As long as it remains only a threat, the violence at the disposal of absolute masculinity feels legitimate—feels, indeed, like the power implicit in legitimacy itself. As a threat, this violence polices the psyche, appearing as guilt, depression, compliance, or constraint within both women and men rather than as the abuse (or worse) of women by men. Only when it is acted out does this violence risk becoming outlaw. The risk, however, is incurred only after the deed of violence is done. In the moment of its enactment, violence against the feminine, violence against women, always feels legitimate to the man who enacts it. That is why it is so readily excused, even by its victims; that is why it is so easily repeated, even by those who feel deeply remorseful at having inflicted it. Built into the very structure of identity, sexual violence is always already sublimated into the inner or outer threat by which it (re)establishes itself as legitimate.

Feminist theories uniting psychoanalysis and semiotics suggest two ways of conceptualizing this state of affairs, one based on Lacan's concept of the phallus and one based on the classical Freudian account of masculine Oedipal subject-formation.[1] Sketches of both schemes follow in due course, outlining the concepts I need in order to pursue my thesis. In the interim, let me suggest the spirit in which these concepts will be used, a suggestion made necessary by the recent resurgence of attacks on psychoanalysis as both unscientific and hostile to women.[2]

This is scarcely the place to mount a detailed apology for psychoanalysis or a critique of the misreadings and misunderstandings that inform much of the case against it.[3] It is, rather, a place to indicate allegiances, which I can do sufficiently (and gratefully) by quoting from the philosopher Thomas Nagel:

> For most of those who believe in the reality of repression and
> the unconscious . . . the belief is based not on blind trust in
> the authority of analysts and their clinical observations but

on the evident usefulness of a rudimentary Freudian outlook in understanding ourselves and other people, particularly erotic life, family dramas, and what Freud called the psychopathology of everyday life. Things that would otherwise surprise us do not; behavior or feelings that would otherwise seem simply irrational become nevertheless comprehensible. You feel miserable all day and then discover that it is the forgotten anniversary of the death of someone who was important to you. . . . Since controlled and reproducible experiments are impracticable here, the kind of internal understanding characteristic of psychoanalysis must rely on the dispersed but cumulative confirmation in life that supports more familiar psychological judgments.

The question is not whether Freud got it exactly right, or whether strong criticism cannot be made of some of his case histories, but whether the types of explanation he introduced substantially amplify the understanding of ourselves and others that common-sense psychology provides. I believe that the pervasive Freudian transformation of our modern working conception of the self is evidence of the validity of his attempt to extend the psychological far beyond its conscious base. Common sense has in fact expanded to include parts of Freudian theory. . . . To many of us it certainly *feels* as if, much of the time, consciousness reveals only the surface of our minds and, for many, this feeling is confirmed by their dreams. (35–36)

It is the intimate linkage between psychoanalysis and the texture of everyday life that allows me to say, following Teresa de Lauretis, that I seek to direct my reflections "not to but through psychoanalysis—to whom it may concern" ("Habit" 311).

The commonsense psychology on offer here situates gender

olarity in a cultural regime of Oedipal or phallic subject-formation that canonizes sexual violence against anything or anyone coded as feminine. Gender polarity occurs when the duality masculine-feminine is constructed around a rigid boundary, a phallic bar or barrier, in terms of mutual exclusion and masculine dominance. My point is not to identify this polarity, which is all too familiar to both its friends and foes, but to suggest its underlying dynamic.

Gender polarity is set in motion when a man's behavior meets (or a woman's accepts or encourages) most or all of three conditions. First, the man claims to occupy the masculine subject-position absolutely rather than relatively: to occupy it, so to speak, as the lender rather than the borrower of the phallus. Second, the "claimer" (Freud's term for a phallic woman, but here referring to men acting as such phallic women are imagined to act) embodies his status as a "borrower" in the person of someone else, someone who, as a woman (or effeminate man) is not even entitled to borrow. Third, the claimer consolidates, in the person of the false, feminine, "borrower," a positive form of his actual lack of entitlement, which he identifies with her femininity. The consolidation may be covert or overt, subtle or crude, verbal or physical. It may work through either idealization or contempt, desire or aggression. It does not, however, work even-handedly. Even the slightest fault line in idealization or desire can provoke contempt or aggression in excess of any apparent reason. Both men and women are notoriously ready to justify or excuse this outcome. ("I shouldn't have, but she was asking for it." "If only I had. . . . If only I hadn't. . . . ") In the order of gender polarity, the ambivalence built into femininity is always skewed toward the negative.

This dynamic is the half-acknowledged subject of Leo Tolstoy's infamous story "The Kreutzer Sonata," the tale of a self-loathing husband, one Pozdnyshev, who murders his wife for her infidelity. Whether the infidelity occurs in a literal sense is moot and really does not matter; the sexual performance is supposedly brought to light by a musical performance but actually consists in that musical performance itself. The music is Beethoven's "Kreutzer" Sonata; it is played, with a passion too great for its salonlike occasion, by the wife at the piano and the down-at-heels son of a bankrupt landowner at the violin. Pozdnyshev sees this violinist, Trukhachevski, as a monstrosity not because he, Trukhachevski, desires Pozdnyshev's wife, but because he resembles her. In Trukhachevski the cultural secret that must be kept at any cost, the incorporation of a feminine position within the structure of masculinity, ceases to be a secret; it becomes transparent, even blatant.

Pozdnyshev's murder of his wife is an impromptu ritual through which this revelation is reconcealed. To make it so, the details of the murder, which are particularly brutal, fall into a symbolic pattern. Pozdnyshev's dagger encounters a resistant substance—both his wife's corset "and something else"—before plunging into "something soft"; the murder is initially a kind of rape. But the result is the production of a striking bloodstain, marked both as the immediate gush of blood from under the corset and, later, as a black stain spread over the wife's discarded dress. The eroticized murder produces the traditional sign of the virtuous wife's deflowering. The resistant "something else" acts as a surrogate hymen; the murder reenacts the original sexual act by which the husband, with or without his wife's consent, ratifies his manhood by legitimately shedding her blood.

"The Kreutzer Sonata" shows gender polarity in its most self-conscious and also its most reprehensible form. The story both says explicitly just what I say here, that sexual violence is the pathology of modern subjectivity, and embodies that pathology in the very act of indicting it. For that reason, and also because of its insight that music is somehow at the heart of the dilemmas of gender polarity, I return to "The Kreutzer Sonata" often in this book.

Other sources furnish other insights. I am also concerned to suggest the dynamic for an alternative to gender polarity, which I call gender synergy. Gender synergy collapses the polarized structures that privilege an abusive virility. It by no means does away with assertive energies, but it does demote them; they cease to be necessary to the articulation of sexual difference, and they circulate freely around and through possible positions instead of belonging exclusively to a single position. At the same time, gender synergy uncouples sexual difference from the heterosexuality that, in the modern era, has come to ground it. The general importance of homosexual desire, even for those who don't act on it, surfaces repeatedly in this book.

Gender synergy occurs when a single subject occupies both masculine and feminine positions either simultaneously or in rhythmic succession, in representation or behavior, in solitude or company, in whole (by cross-identification, literal or figurative cross-dressing) or in part (by redistributing the traits characteristic of each position). The result is the ability to affirm that authority, truth, and pleasure inhere in the ad hoc ensemble of positions rather than in a fixed and prepotent masculine position.

The word *affirm* is important here, because all gender synergies can be interpreted in terms that reduce them to expressions of gender polarity. The reason for this reductive possibility is that gender polarity is basic to the order of the culture we have inherited. Synergy can only emerge from within the framework of polarity, and the practice of synergy is correspondingly fraught with dangers and anxiety even for those most drawn to it. In this book, for instance: most of the examples of synergy are male-authored and therefore open to challenge as appropriations of femininity. The conviction that they are something more and better can emerge only if they appear to release a centrifugal energy that no mere fixed position can control. For that to happen, the energy must be both potential in the gesture of synergy itself and kinetic in the response of an interpreter, who must, by improvising the necessary language and rhythm of thought, reperform the gesture so that its synergy is credible. The vitality of gender synergy consists precisely in its ability to prompt or embody an interpretation that can defer the reinstatement of the polarized norm.

For this reason gender synergy is not to be confused with either "gender-bending" by role-reversal (the technique of inversion) or androgynous "gender-blending," although elements of both may appear within a given act of synergy.[4] Inversion and androgyny function less as alternatives to gender polarity than as unruly forms of it; they represent a relocating or reordering of polarized terms. Synergy must do more; it must disperse and deconstruct those terms. Nonetheless, synergy cannot be distinguished from inversion or androgyny by rule or by rote. There is no set of formal properties unique to any of these practices; the differences between them are practical, context-sensitive, dependent on interpretation. We might even say, drawing on the principle that synergies can always be reduced to expressions of polarity, that synergy unravels from the moment we begin to "read it down" into inversion or androgyny.

An odd couple of nineteenth-century poets, Walt Whitman and Alfred Tennyson, respectable Bohemian and (im)proper Victorian, were galvanized by gender synergy and wrote at white heat under its promptings. Whitman was a prototypical "gay" poet who nonetheless wrote memorably—and notoriously—about genital love between men and women: "limitless limpid jets of love hot and enormous, quivering jelly of love, white-blow and delirious juice" ("I Sing the Body Electric" l. 59). Tennyson was an officially "straight" poet whose most important work was an elegy celebrating his meltingly eroticized love for another man: "Descend, and touch, and enter; hear / The wish too strong for words to name" (*In Memoriam 93*). Whitman longs for both masculine and feminine intimacies and does not much care whose body conveys them; one of his most arresting images, from "I Sing the Body Electric," interweaves the presence of a tender nursing mother with that of a ruggedly virile patriarch:

> He drank water only, the blood show'd like scarlet through
>   the clear-brown skin of his face,
> He was a frequent gunner and fisher, he sail'd his boat
>   himself, he had a fine one presented to him by a ship-
>   joiner, he had fowling-pieces presented to him by men that
>   loved him,
> When he went with his five sons and many grand-sons to
>   hunt or fish, you would pick him out as the most beautiful
>   and vigorous of the gang,

You would wish long and long to be with him, you would
   wish to sit by him in the boat that you and he might touch
   each other.

ll. 41–44

The beautiful old man is both a paradigm of manly action and a
site of immobile caressing presence, a phallic master engorged
with blood and a circulator of vital nourishing fluids, a figure of
pure self-possession and one through whom gifts, be they objects
or touches, are given and taken. Tennyson similarly imagines his
friend Arthur Hallam as a male mother, a source of liquescent
bliss yet a virile culture hero; and he imagines himself as a male
wife, meekly worshipful and yet a virile poet.

It is no accident that these examples of synergy come, like my
examples of polarity, from the nineteenth century. The period in
which the Western bourgeoisie achieved its historical triumph is
also the period in which our modern oppositions of masculinity
and femininity, heterosexuality and homosexuality, were formed.
The work of Michel Foucault has shown what should, perhaps,
have been always before our eyes: that the "repression" of sexuality in the nineteenth century cannot be taken at face value, that
it is part of a larger social process, a general sexualization of life,
a "putting of sex into discourse," that continues unabated today.
Even in an accelerating state of collapse, the nineteenth-century
gender system still sets our agendas as subjects. The formative
years of this system offer more revealing, more candid representations of both polarity and synergy than more recent times can
generally offer—certainly more than is offered by the modernist
era, which so often interpreted an enhanced misogyny and ho-

mophobia as the vehicle of cultural heroism.[5] We no longer accept nineteenth-century preachments, but that does not stop us from practicing what the nineteenth century preached. More even than to the culture in which they came to life, the focal texts of this book belong to the culture of their afterlife, the culture that continuously revives them as classics. In which form, misrecognized, in fragments, displaced or condensed, they become part of a shared textual unconscious, part of the stuff that dreams are made on—not least my own. So the best way to envision a new gender system for the next century may well be to reenvision the system that was new in the last.

Best, that is, if I am right in thinking that our best hope for a humane gender system, an unsystematic system in which coercion has no place and improvisation is everyplace, lies in the critique of gender polarity and the practice of gender synergy. This book is meant to advance the critique and inspire the practice. These aims, however, will be somewhat assymetrical, correlative to the assymetry in power and status between men and women. The critique of gender polarity is basic to feminist thought, and this book, any book, can do no more than put a new element into play in a very rich conceptual field. In this case, the new element is a model of the underlying dynamic of gender polarity. But gender synergy is different. When women practice it, they assume privileges historically denied to them; when men practice it, they surrender—or, better, repudiate—privileges historically reserved for them. It follows that gender synergy cannot establish itself culturally unless men come to embrace it, and that not grudgingly or resignedly but with enthusiasm.

This book, accordingly, is addressed differently to men and to women. Women, of course, have been articulating the problems of gender difference and violence for a long time; they have said loud and clear that, as Dorothy Dinerstein put it, "what women want is to stop serving as scapegoats (their own scapegoats as well as men's and children's scapegoats) for human resentment of the human condition" (234). If Dinerstein's answer to Freud's famous "What do women want?" is right, then this book is meant to show that men can share women's desire, can need an end to the scapegoating, can demand the replacement of resentment by the shared recognition of human limits. To this end, the book presents a dialogue of masculinities and femininities by a male author, and mostly about male authors, in which phallic polarity seeks to overcome itself and metamorphose into a fluid, uncoercive duality that can also unexpectedly become a unity or a plurality. It tries to locate an actual, viable masculinity that does not merely seek to appropriate the feminine as a part of itself or as a means of representing masculine desires and ideals.

For men, the book sketches a practice of masculine identity that may include phallic, firmly bounded, and agonistic elements without being limited to them or by them, without demanding that they be unambivalent, and without requiring a feminine or feminized Other against which (violently) to privilege them. This mobile masculinity, moreover, seeks to be equally accessible to both straight and gay men, but its embrace—again, not reluctant, but free and wholehearted—requires that straight men cast out not only misogyny but also homophobia, whether directed against gay men or lesbian women. Homosexualities, arguably a product and certainly a vehicle of social resistance to gender polarity, offer models of gender synergy from which anyone, however disposed to feel or act on same-sex desire, can benefit.

True to its theme, this book is itself a kind of synergy, a network or constellation of reflections based primarily on the material mentioned and implied so far: the novella by Tolstoy and the music by Beethoven it names; the poetry of a gay writer, Whitman, and his straight counterpart, Tennyson; and the primal scene of the lovedeath, both within opera and without. From these nuclei of concern a pattern of interpretation branches out on a variety of collateral materials. To the depth I hope to gain from intensive focus on Tolstoy and Beethoven, Tennyson and Whitman, love in death and death in love, a breadth should emerge as this focus impels itself to widen. There are readings of other exemplary nineteenth-century works, reflections on the character of polarity and synergy, and comments on notable recent events—the names Bobbitt and Simpson could hardly be left out of a study like this. There are even interpretations of three of my own dreams—a Freudian strategy based partly on my conviction that in some sense it was this series of dreams that taught me, before I was aware of it, the thesis of this book. The dreams, like the most famous dream of the twentieth century, the "primal scene" dream of the patient Freud called the Wolf Man, all concern themselves with wolves, woods, windows, and desire.

Taken together, my readings offer a prismatic anatomy of both the sexual violence sanctioned in the cultural order of gender and a nonviolent gendering of the human subject that may, just may, follow from disordering that order in all its senses. Admittedly, and obviously, these readings cannot "prove" my thesis about polarity and synergy as if it were an experimental hypothesis. My anatomies are interpretive rather than empirical, products of a thought experiment energized rather than inhibited by the friction of differences, the crossing of conceptual borders, the leaps of faith between speculation and reality. It would be naive, however, to think that this procedure unfolds at a safe distance from the misogyny of everyday life and the brutalities of actual harassment, abuse, battery, and rape. On the contrary, it is precisely in the realm of representation, of images charged with value, pressure, feeling, images recognized and misrecognized, conscious and unconscious, that actual sexual violence is grounded and in which its antidote must likewise be grounded. When men abuse women they act from a sense of entitlement: they do what a man has a right to do. The sense, the right, may be abhorrent, but it is too pervasive to be explained away as abnormal. Rather it honors the norm of a cultural order in which gender polarity, precisely because it is never quite true, must compulsively reestablish itself as the truth. Corpus delicti.

One more note on method. In taking shape as a synergy based on a small body of material, this book becomes a palimpsest or tapestry of case histories: studies of particulars in which the typical reveals itself so fully that the particular itself becomes general, "exemplary" in every sense of the term, a contingent happening that in retrospect seems necessary. The case history reveals what Whitman called "facts showered over with light"; it finds the angles of vision, the levels of discourse, from which, as Goethe claimed, "Everything factual is, in a sense, theory. . . . There is no sense in looking for something behind phenomena: they *are* theory."[6] There is, of course, no gainsaying that the choice of material for these case histories is to some degree arbitrary. But a text like this gains credibility by assembling possibilities rather than by demonstrating necessities. The process is like composing a theme and variations: the choice of theme is arbitrary but gains credibility insofar as it serves to show the possibilities of variation, transformation, and thereby insight. In my own "variations," I have sought both to gain intensivity by recurring continually to the exemplary figures of Beethoven, Tolstoy, Tennyson, and Whitman, and to gain breadth by branching out freely to reflect on a variety of "satellite" texts, topics, and events.

Oedipus Tyrannos (Swellfoot the Tyrant)

Post-Freudian psychoanalysis has by and large balked at the central position that Freud accorded to the Oedipus complex. As Freud took a certain pleasure in insisting, the Oedipus complex is bad news. It is bad news because it places transgressive desire at a major node of human development, a fact that led American ego psychology to sanitize the human subject that this development produces. It is bad news because it inscribes in subjectivity the authority of the bourgeois family, a fact that led Gilles Deleuze and Felix Guattari in their *Anti-Oedipus* to scourge all things Oedipal on behalf of unstructured "schiz-flows" of desire, one victim of their assault being the hapless messenger, psychoanalysis itself. The Oedipus complex is bad news because it authorizes and perpetuates the oppression of women, a fact that leads some feminist analysts and critics to delve into pre-Oedipal formations in order to recover the countervailing figure of the mother.[7] And the news gets worse. It can be compellingly argued that the underlying dynamic of narrative, the most ubiquitous of

literary forms as of sense-making activities in general, is funda-
mentally Oedipal in character, that the function of narrative is to
project the formation of the human subject in culture as normatively masculine in relation to a field of femininity that he seeks
to traverse, overcome, or possess.[8]

It is no wonder, then, that those of us who are working to
change the face of this subject and to unravel the ideologies that
support it must all become anti-Oedipus. In this respect, our
most distinguished predecessor is, of all people, Sigmund Freud.
For although Freud does tend, in varying degrees, to endorse the
social values that underlie the psychical structures his theories
describe, he also stands as the most subversive antagonist those
values have yet had. It is Freud who is the first anti-Oedipal
thinker, even if he is not a wholly evenhanded one. It was Freud
the famous misogynist who wrote:

> [Women's] training excludes them from occupying them-
> selves intellectually with regard to sexual problems, in regard
> to which they naturally have the greatest thirst for knowl-
> edge, and terrifies them with the pronouncement that such
> curiosity is unwomanly and a sign of immoral tendencies.
> And thus they are thoroughly intimidated from all mental ef-
> fort, and knowledge in general is depreciated in their eyes.
> The prohibition of knowledge extends beyond the sexual
> sphere . . . acting precisely in the same way as the prohibition
> of religious speculation among men, and the taboo of any
> thought out of harmony with loyalty in faithful subjects.
>
> *"'Civilized' Sexual Morality"* 35–36

The indictment of mental constraint in this passage is unsparing,
and so is the recognition of sexual injustice. Freud suggests that
feminine ignorance is positionally equivalent to masculine ortho-

doxy and subservience in the general order of constraint. But he also sees that it is women whose constraint is the greater, because it imposes a double loss: that of knowing pleasure, and that of the pleasure in knowing.

It is, however, more typical for Freud to hone in on the damage that Oedipal dynamics do to men—men like himself. And in voicing this half of the anti-Oedipal critique, a half that, as we will see, implicates the other half as well, Freud also speaks for other men formed in the nineteenth century for whom patriarchal culture—Oedipal culture—was at once an incontestable given and a site of both conscious and unconscious contestation.

In its fully theorized form, as articulated in Freud's *The Ego and the Id* (1923), the Oedipus complex lays down the basic structure of both identity formation and cultural transmission. The subject shaped by this structure is, normatively, that of the little boy; the fact that girls do not fit the pattern is both a theoretical problem that Freud saw clearly and a cultural problem to which he was generally blind. In renouncing the mother and introjecting the father, who then becomes the core of his superego, the little boy both consolidates his character around a masculine image and subjects himself to the patriarchal authority of culture. (Freud argues that the boy will simultaneously play this scenario with roles reversed, renouncing the father and introjecting the mother; before the recent work of Kaja Silverman, however, the implications of this reversal were rarely pursued, least of all by the Oedipal sons who are instructed to repress it.) In return for his compliance, an abnegation severe enough that Jacques Lacan equates it to castration, the Oedipal son is promised that he, too, will one day stand in the position of the Oedipal father.[9]

Even on this cursory description, the Oedipal regime is clearly built on violence. Its violence, indeed, is double. First, it arrests the boy's free circulation among different subject-positions, positions he assumes by identifying with various aspects of both his mother and his father as well as of other caretakers. The Oedipus complex centers on a single subject-position, around which it constructs what is meant to be a fixed, implacably gendered identity. A plural character, which Freud sometimes called the pleasure-ego, is succeeded by a dual character consisting of an official ego and an authoritative superego. This change is not an evolution but a break, the symbolic repetition of which is a primary means for maintaining the psychic and ideological identity of the Oedipal subject. For psychoanalysis, subject-formation begins when the orientation of the infant shifts from biological need to psychological desire, from the demands of the body to the fantasies of the pleasure-ego.[10] The Oedipus complex abruptly curtails this movement, appropriating and regulating it in the paternal name of culture.

Second, with identity fixed under (and by) its authority, the superego becomes highly aggressive, repeatedly punishing the ego for the primal crimes (parricide and incest) that were never, in fact, committed. In Freud's words, the superego "can be super-moral and then become cruel as only the id can be. . . . [Thus] even ordinary normal morality has a harshly restraining, cruelly prohibiting quality" (*Ego* 44).

What is probably Freud's sharpest indictment of the Oedipal regime occurs in the late essay "Dostoyevsky and Parricide" (1928). Assessing Dostoyevsky as a moralist, Freud accuses him of a great betrayal:

After the most violent struggles to reconcile the instinctual demands of the individual with the claims of the community, he landed in the retrograde position of submission both to temporal and spiritual authority, of veneration both for the Czar and for the God of the Christians . . . —a position which lesser minds have reached with smaller effort. . . . Dostoyevsky threw away the chance of becoming a teacher and liberator of humanity and made himself one with their jailers. The future of civilization will have little to thank him for. (275)

The ground of this moral failure is said to be an Oedipal struggle that accentuates the problem of what Freud elsewhere calls moral masochism ("Economic Problem"). Dostoyevsky's father, like his novelistic counterpart Fyodor Karamazov, was unusually "hard, violent, and cruel" (283), and his chief legacy to his son was a superego with the same qualities. In order to defend himself against this superego, Dostoyevsky sought to win its love by adopting a passive, feminine attitude toward it. The (masculine) sadism of the superego found its complement in the (feminine) masochism of the ego.

In relation to subject-formation in general, this strategy might be written off as pathological, even bizarre, but Freud will not have it so. "The normal processes," he writes, "in the formation of conscience must be similar to the abnormal ones described here. We have not yet succeeded in fixing the boundary line between them. It will be observed that here the largest share in the event is ascribed to the passive component of repressed femininity" ("Dostoyevsky" 283). Taken together with Freud's adverse judgment of Dostoyevsky, this statement tersely issues a critique of Oedipal subject-formation that can be put in the form of three propositions. First, the "normal" Oedipus complex is implicated in, and perhaps inextricable from, impressions of sadistic abuse. (These impressions may take the form of memories, fantasies, or a blend of both.) Second, culture tends to maintain its authority by sublimating and idealizing such impressions (e.g., in the service of the Czar or the Christian God). Third, the psychocultural position of femininity is constituted above all as the object of this abusive authority.

The last point is the most far-reaching in its implications. Femininity is not put into play in order to serve the interests of women, but in order to provide the superego and its institutions with a paradigmatic figure of compliance. For Oedipal sons, the social subject-position inscribed as masculine is paired with a psychical position inscribed as feminine. Oedipal daughters, in turn, are compelled to personify the feminine position in the social world. Strange though it may sound, the Oedipal son represents the normalized version of a favorite nineteenth-century pathological type, the sexual "invert" said to bear a woman's spirit in a man's body (*anima muliebris virili corpore inclusa*). Normal masculinity arises when the woman's spirit cross-dresses as a man's. Freud thus sees the Oedipal scenario steadily and sees it whole, and he does not like what he sees.

A Little Extra Piece

As its title implies, this is a section devoted to the phallus.

The Oedipal regime is phallic by both compulsion and inclination, but it is important not to misunderstand what this means. Insistence on the phallus has been taken as a sign of misogyny in

both Freud and Lacan, and also as itself a phallic gesture of theoretical mastery. There is truth in both claims. But the truth re-
flects a risk that needs to be taken; there is no way to undo the
regime of the phallus without understanding how it works. Insistence on the phallus is easy to overdo, but done sensibly it is
simply candor about historical circumstances. As Ellie Raglund-
Sullivan says of Lacan in particular, it is hard to fault him for
pointing out the obvious (284).

It is Lacan, moreover, who for all his obscurantism, is most
helpful on the subject. More clearly than Freud ever did, Lacan
detaches the phallus as a signifier from the penis to which it necessarily alludes. As a signifier, part of a culturally instituted system of signs, the phallus can claim no natural authority. It is always a construction, a fiction, a kind of stage prop. Recognizing
this enables Lacan to recognize that the phallus cannot escape
from ambivalence. It has a dual character—the very thing that,
as the signifier of subjective unity and integrity, it ought to
transcend.

What are the terms of this duality? On the one hand, the phallus is the mark of cultural and psychical supremacy. It betokens
the autonomy of the self and the power to achieve *jouissance*—
bliss, enjoyment, entitlement, orgasm, a pleasure beyond representation originally based on union with the mother. Given the
power and position of the superego and its cultural institutions,
claims to possess the phallus in this sense must always be false.
Still, if executed deftly they will always be believed by both oneself and others. On the other hand, the phallus only enters discourse in relation to castration, which is to say in relation to the
possibility of its loss and, concurrently, the inaccessibility of what
it signifies. The phallus is therefore the mark of absence, of in-

sufficiency, of desire without the power of gratification. Claims to possess the phallus in this sense may sometimes be true, but no one ever makes them.

This duality in the phallus accords, perhaps a little too neatly, with the contrastive "orders" or "registers" in which Lacan situates the human psyche.[11] The imaginary, the order of fantasy and identification, offers the positive phallus; the symbolic, the order of language and law, offers the negative one. The logic of sexual violence can be said to turn on the effort to translate the symbolic into the imaginary phallus. This effort may succeed in the short run, but not in the long—just the wrong arithmetic for a phallus. Make it your own as much as you like, the imaginary phallus must always be given up, always submit or resubmit to castration. Yet the game can always be played again, to the point of becoming compulsive, on the strength of the illusion that, next time, or the time after that, one can turn the trick.

My thesis is that what counts as normal masculine subjectivity involves a continual effort to defer the arrival, which is to say the return, of the castratory moment. Sexual violence is the deferral technique of last resort. It does not represent a break with the norm, but the norm's logical outcome.

Sexual violence is precipitated when the awareness of one's negative condition—that one does not possess the phallus, after all, and never can—assumes a haunting positive form, an apparitional form. One sees or hears something that makes one queasy; one feels pressed to recognize that the phallus belongs to someone else, and always has, and rightly, even when one seemed to wield it with utter self-assurance. This someone else is not the generalized Other that Lacan identifies with the symbolic order. It is someone else in particular. And yet, maddeningly, this someone else almost never appears in his own person. He hides behind a symbol, a persona, or an emissary—the last typically a woman—who mercilessly exposes one's imposture. No one is spared the tyranny of this impalpable other man, who can equally well take on concrete, monstrous form (Goya's Saturn, blood running from his mouth as he gnaws off the head of the son he devours) or remain only an impalpable nameless phantom:

> As if a phantom caress'd me,
> I thought I was not alone walking here by the shore;
> But the one I thought was with me as now I walk by the
>   shore, the one I lov'd that caress'd me,
> As I lean and look through the glimmering light, that one has
>   utterly disappear'd,
> And those appear that are hateful to me and mock me.
>
> *Whitman, "As If a Phantom Caress'd Me"*

This poem records the process of dispossession: the fantasy of sudden reversal in which one becomes the object of hatred and mockery at the very place where one thought oneself the subject of love and respect. Anything can trigger such a fantasy; the pretext can be weighty or trivial, intentional or unintentional. As to what the fantasy triggers in its turn: unless the man who thinks himself dispossessed can identify some token of conciliation or compensation, the outcome may well be violence. It may well be violence anyway.

"Any man has to, wants to, needs to"

In relation to his wife, as he tells us repeatedly, Tolstoy's Pozdnyshev acts like all men of his social class, the landed gentry.
In relation to women in general, haunted by "woman, every
woman, woman's nudity" (366) he acts like all men: "nine-tenths,
if not more, not of our class only but of all classes, even the peas-
ants" (367). He is an absolutely typical figure; his individuality
seems to consist of nothing but the excessiveness of his typicality,
even when his typical rage at his wife vents itself in her murder.
Yet this absolutely typical man has become something absolutely
exceptional. Remorse over the murder has transformed him into
an uncanny figure. He has become a charismatic stranger on a
train, Coleridge's Ancient Mariner as a chain-smoking modern
neurotic, complete with a vocal tic, a strange tale to tell, and glittering eyes that rivet the listener-victim to the telling. The listener, who serves as a frame narrator for "The Kreutzer Sonata,"

is a fellow passenger on a railway journey who makes several
failed attempts to engage Pozdnyshev in conversation. In the end,
as with the Ancient Mariner, the initiative comes from the side
of remorse and the uncanny. Compare:

> We heard, behind me, a sound like that of a broken laugh or
> sob; and on turning round we saw my neighbor, the lonely
> gray-haired man with the glittering eyes, who had
> approached unnoticed during our conversation. . . . He stood
> with his arms on the back of the seat, evidently much agi-
> tated; his face was red and a muscle twitched in his cheek.

> [To the frame narrator:] "Would you like me to tell you
> [alone] how . . . love led to what happened to me?". . . .
>   I repeated that I wished it very much. He paused, rubbed
> his face with his hands, and began:
>   "If I am to tell it, I must tell everything from the
> beginning."
>
> "Kreutzer" 360, 364

> It is an Ancient Mariner,
> And he stoppeth one of three.
> "By thy long gray beard and glittering eye
> Now wherefore stopp'st thou me?". . . .

> He holds him with his skinny hand,
> "There was a ship," quoth he. . . .

> The Wedding-Guest sat on a stone:
> He cannot chuse but hear.

And thus spake on that ancient man,
That bright-eyed Mariner.

> *"Rime of the Ancient Mariner"*
> *ll. 1–4, 8–10, 16–20*

Other figures of nineteenth-century masculine iconography also lurk in Pozdnyshev's shadow. The Flying Dutchman, the Wandering Jew, the Byronic hero: each one is a personification of the utter insider's dread and desire of being utterly on the outside.

The value of such a figure is supposed to lie in his no longer being the man he was. Pozdnyshev narrates the story of his sexual violence, which is the story of his typicality, precisely when he is no longer typical, after he has undergone the "spiritual conversion" that (again like the Ancient Mariner's) makes him a spellbinding storyteller. Yet he still loves and compassionates the man he was; his narrative shows it at every turn. Distanced from his former self in principle, he is in practice constantly intimate with it. He identifies with it as a reader does with a character, or as the frame narrator identifies with him. When Pozdnyshev narrates the events surrounding his wife's murder, the gripping immediacy of his tale invites the frame narrator—invites us—to abandon all sense of critical distance. Male or female, with or without our consent, we are drawn into imagining the killing from the killer's point of view. We are seduced by the character's theatrical-aesthetic pleasure in acting the role of murderer and by his erotic-narcissistic pleasure in making the role a reality. It is no wonder that the frame narrator ends the story with an expression of sympathy for Pozdnyshev, not for his victim:

> I touched him with my hand. He uncovered his face, and I could not see if he had been asleep.

'Good-bye,' I said, holding out my hand. He gave me his
and smiled slightly, but so piteously that I felt ready to weep.

'Yes, forgive me . . . ' he said, repeating the same words
with which he had concluded his story. (428)

Sadder but wiser, the frame narrator gives the grieving killer a
token of forgiveness that is also a token of affection. Unless we're
careful, we readers, we will let him do it as our surrogate.

The Bathers

In one of the most beautiful sections of "Song of Myself," Walt Whitman imagines a young woman watching from a window while twenty-eight young men swim naked in the sea. At one level this scene is a means for Whitman to attach explicitly erotic masculine desire to male bodies. The young woman becomes his pretext, indeed his instrument, for performing imaginary fellatio on the young men:

> Where are you off to, lady? for I see you,
> You splash in the water there, yet stay stock-still in your
>   room.
>
> Dancing and laughing along the beach came the twenty-
>   ninth bather,
> The rest did not see her, but she saw them and loved
>   them. . . .
> The young men float on their backs, their white bellies bulge
>   to the sun, they do not ask who seizes fast to them,

> They do not know who puffs and declines with pendant and
>   bending arch,
> They do not think whom they souse with spray.
>
> ll. 206–9, 214–16

The poetry flushes with homoerotic lyricism as the rhythmic ebb and flow of the verse mirrors its counterpart in the sea that envelops the blissful bodies and sets them free.

The woman, though, remains decidedly in the picture. She is someone seen as well as the source of the eye through which one sees. She is no mere pretext but a real presence, not a curb on same-sex desire but a surplus that spills over from it. Whitman takes pains to imagine her circumstances, her longings, her enforced sexual ignorance; he associates her desire with the twenty-eight phases of the moon, and therefore with the rhythms of both menstruation and the tides. Hence the woman is also a vehicle by which Whitman can experience what he construes as feminine desire. She grants him the imaginary privilege of experiencing her body as his own.

The intricate, unfixed role of the desiring woman renders this passage an exemplary study in gender synergy. Both the dynamics of desire and the sense of identity are involved. The object of desire becomes multiple, and more than that, multiple in principle. Those desired become interchangeable, yet the subject's desire is for each of them personally, and is far too tender to be dehumanizing. As if to suggest a counterpart to Luce Irigaray's epigram, "women have sex organs just about everywhere" (*This Sex* 28), the synergized subject proves to have objects of desire in just about everyone. No less multiple, or multiform, is the subject's desire itself. It is both diffuse (directed at the whole person) and concentrated (directed at the bulging bellies, at once an image of pregnancy inscribed on the male body and of displaced penile swelling). It is both visual (evolved from a voyeuristic position) and nonvisual (evolved into a fantasy of being in the scene observed). Finally, it is both promiscuous and chaste. Its rich satisfaction is available to the desiring subject without actual touch; synergized sex can be imaginary without loss or sacrifice. As to the sense of identity, the subject of desire here is simultaneously and authentically both masculine and feminine but not synthetically androgynous. Embodied by the young woman but not identical with her, loving the beautiful swimmers both homosexually and heterosexually, the subject is a composite, a confederation of masculine and feminine characteristics and positions.

Brimstone

Here is an impassioned denunciation of gender polarity: "The education of women will always correspond with men's opinion toward them. . . . [Woman] is a means of enjoyment. Her body is a means of enjoyment. And she knows this. It is just as it is with slavery. . . . The enslavement of woman lies simply in the fact that people desire, and think it good, to avail themselves of her as a tool of enjoyment." The work of a nineteenth-century feminist? Not at all. Gender polarity at its sharpest produces an obsessional interest in its own structure that approaches (but never quite becomes) self-critique. Thus it is an *anti*-feminist, tortured by a terror of female sexuality so great that he feels his identity collapsing into the disgusting liquefaction of his own desire, who writes so incisively about the oppression of women under patriarchy. It is Tolstoy, in "The Kreutzer Sonata" (384–85).

A Whole Piece More

Freud recounts an anecdote in *The Psychopathology of Everyday Life* that beautifully epitomizes the cultural history of the phallus—both the long and the short of it:

A man of twenty-four has preserved the following picture from his fifth year. He is sitting in the garden of a summer villa, on a small chair beside his aunt, who is trying to teach him the letters of the alphabet. He is in difficulties over the difference between *m* and *n* and he asks his aunt to tell him how to know one from the other. His aunt points out that the *m* has a whole piece more than the *n*—the third stroke. There appeared to be no reason for challenging the trustworthiness of this childhood memory; it had, however, only acquired its meaning at a later date, when it showed itself suited to represent symbolically another of the boy's curiosities. For just as at that time he wanted to know the difference between *m* and *n*, so later he was anxious to find out the difference between boys and girls, and would have been very

willing for this particular aunt to be the one to teach him. He
also discovered then that the difference was a similar one—
that a boy, too, has a whole piece more than a girl; and at the
time when he acquired this piece of knowledge he called up
the recollection of the parallel curiosity of his childhood.
(48–49)

Freud's insight here is indebted to the culturally motivated confusion he shares with the inquisitive young man. This is the confusion between lack of visibility and absence.[12] If we undo that
confusion, if we recognize that one may have something one cannot show, then what a boy "has" is not a whole piece more than
a girl, but the prized, fantasmatically charged capacity to show
himself as he stands, in two senses, erect. The identification of
having with showing leads to a further identification of having
with knowing, as Freud's language suggests; when the young
man learns the function of his "whole piece more" in articulating sexual difference, what he acquires is a whole "piece" of
knowledge.

From these confusions, much follows.

First, manhood is defined as a wholeness, an intactness, an integrity of self. In effect, this definition provides the model for the
famous image of "man" as microcosm. The wholeness of nature
is represented in the wholeness of the psyche, which in turn is
represented in the wholeness of the virile body, which in turn
is represented in the wholeness of the extra piece by which the
masculine exceeds the feminine. Yet at the same time, this wholeness gives a disproportionate value to the piece, to the part rather
than to the whole. It is the part that anchors the concentric series
of wholes. It is the part that, in its vulnerability—ironically at one

with its visibility—constantly poses the danger of collapsing the microcosmic structure into a whirlpool, a concentric series of holes.

Second, manhood is linked with mastery over writing. The outcome of that mastery is a self-knowledge and self-possession that parallels the discovery of one's whole piece more. Mastery over writing frees the virile self from tutelage to a woman and makes that woman available as an object of virile desire. The identification of the extra piece with a stroke of the pen identifies masculine identity with cultural authority. At the same time, the truth of that authority is always already written on the male body in the form of the extra stroke. The authority becomes available in the very instant that the virile subject learns to recognize what his body signifies.

Third, this masculine endowment can nonetheless be conferred only by a woman, only by the inferior being who lacks the whole piece more. And one is "very willing" that this should be so: willing, because the woman, this so-desirable "aunt" in her Edenic summer garden, masks or defers the presence of her formidable masculine counterpart, the full-sized other male who turns the assymetry of a boy's desire for an adult woman into a permanent disability. What the woman really gives the boy is not the phallus, but a kind of phallic prosthesis, and with it the need to pass off this surrogate, this truly extra piece, as the real thing.

Violence and Misrecognition

One consequence of the processes of subject-formation that Freud describes is that the superego puts the masculine subject under contradictory mandates. Freud glosses them as the injunctions to be like and not to be like the Father (here already a symbolic figure, not a person); Kaja Silverman, reading Freud, glosses them as the injunctions to identify with and to be loved by the Father.[13] These contradictions tend to play themselves out along lines suggested by Jacques Lacan's concept of misrecognition, which also indicates their larger context. Lacan is again helpful because he places psychoanalysis firmly in the realm of language, discourse, and therefore culture, whereas Freud vacillates between cultural formation and natural law as the site of analytic truth.

Lacan (or Lacanians like Silverman and Slavoj Žižek) draws attention to the way that representations become illusions or even fetishes: the way, for instance, that the look of masculine desire misrecognizes itself as the gaze of mastery, or the unpredictably (im)potent penis thinks (so to speak) that it is the all-powerful phallus. These illusions represent the subject's means of addressing, and at the same time defending against, that which Lacan calls The Thing. The Thing (*Das Ding*, a concept derived from Kant's *Ding-an-sich*, the thing in itself) is that which is most real for the subject. It is that which holds out the *jouissance* that the subject claims to desire, but that can actually be experienced only as the subject's annihilation. Misrecognition is the substitution of charismatic things for The Thing. It can occur in either the register of the imaginary, where narcissistic identification and fantasy rule, or the register of the symbolic, where the Father's law and the desires it both prohibits and elicits rule. The symbolic, although it is the subject's "proper" register, never entirely surmounts either the imaginary or the real of The Thing. The imaginary offers "islands of enjoyment" that enchant the subject by their seeming proximity to The Thing. (Žižek suggests that The Thing is above all a mirage seen from those islands.[14]) The symbolic disenchants the imaginary replacements for *jouissance*, but it does so only in order to recover them in an alienated form, as belonging to the Other rather than to the self. This process even applies to the phallus. In its imaginary form the phallus is something one can have (like the father); it is the key to absolute masculine presence. But in its symbolic form the phallus is something that one can only lose (unlike the father); it is the mark of castration, the key to the absolute masculinity, the subjective integrity, that is always the Other's.

Lacanian thinking has tended to emphasize the falsity of misrecognitions and of the social orders that foster them. My purpose here is to emphasize their truth. Although the gaze is always would-be, as the phallus is, the social reality of the gaze is coercively real-enough, as is that of the phallus. The conceptual recognition of an illusion must not be allowed to obscure the pragmatic force of illusion taken for reality, signs taken for wonders. And as with the phallus, breakage of the would-be gaze is a trigger for violence, just as violence is taken as a reasonable means to secure or defend the illusion of the gaze.

(Coup de) Grace Notes

Why did Tolstoy seize in particular on Beethoven's "Kreutzer" Sonata? Perhaps because it embodied a contradiction for him. Its genre, the duo for violin and piano, had not yet been fully professionalized in the 1890s. In genre, the piece is still salon music. But its substance, or rather the substance of the first movement, is nothing of the kind, and the contrast inevitably expresses itself in gendered terms. Just listen to the extravagance of this music, the emotional abundance of its Baroque introduction, the passionate, utterly relentless dynamism of the main sonata form! When I teach the Tolstoy story with the sonata, even students who know nothing of classical music are dazzled by these things. Tolstoy is dead right to stress the music's explosive incongruity: the way its importation of formal monumentality and emotional ferocity into the salon medium suggests the workings of an incommensurable force, something presocialized and unsocializable, that threatens to erupt amid polite conversation, and, more dangerously, to erupt there from within.

From the traditional perspective of the musicologist, this suggestion of uncanny power can be sublimated—sublimated all too easily, so that it disappears or, failing that, becomes merely "subjective"—into the effect of aesthetic success. Thus Charles Rosen writes that the first movement of the "Kreutzer" Sonata is "unequalled in formal clarity, grandeur, and dramatic force by anything Beethoven had yet written" (399). But Tolstoy is deaf to such sublimation, and rightly so. Even though what he makes of what he hears is repugnant, he is right to hear critical and even destructive energy in this music. He is right to hear this energy exposing and attacking a social order built around a dissembled commerce in male desires and female bodies: "how can that first Presto be played in a drawing room among ladies in low-necked dresses? To hear that played, to clap a little, and then to eat ices and talk of the latest scandal?" ("Kreutzer" 411).

A Portmanteau

Neither Tennyson nor Whitman can be parsed strictly as either straight or gay, though each inclines in a different direction. What binds them together and sets them in counterpoint against Tolstoy is their commitment to a powerfully emotional form of masculine companionship—"manly love," as Whitman called it—that, like music, destabilizes gender polarity. (Like music: they, too, hear music this way, but they hear it gladly.) Perhaps we need a new category for men and women with such a disposition, those whose "own" gender identity is only a point of departure, whether they wish it so consistently (Whitman) or only in conflict with a desire to restabilize it (Tennyson): not straights, not gays, but strays.

The First Wolf Dream (1951)

A pack of wolves enters the back alley that leads to the porch of my house, an elevated wooden structure with a small enclosed rose garden at its base. I am identified with the lead wolf, who is looking intently at the bedroom window; I am also in bed, asleep. The dream ends with a voiceover: "Will the wolves succeed in their [unintelligible]. Tune in next week . . . " I am the narrator, although I do not recognize the voice. This is not a nightmare; its chief feelings are vividness and narrative suspense. For weeks afterward I hope to finish the dream and find out if the wolves succeed, but the dream remains unfinished.

The wolves carry an association with Jack London's novel *The Call of the Wild*, some version of which I must have seen on television—hence the voiceover. (The association definitely belongs to my childhood, although it may postdate the dream; I read *The Call of the Wild* at age twelve because I was curious about its bearing on what I had dreamed at five.) The allusion to television, and in particular to the narrative formula of serial adventure ("tune in next week"), is also important in its own right—as important, indeed, as the image of the wolves. Saturday-morning adventure programs were a rich source of fantasies to me at the time, in an unbookish household, and they were also a source of transgression; I secretly used to let our neighbor's children watch them with me, in violation of the Jewish sabbath they were supposed to observe.

The wolves thus signify on two levels. First, they suggest wildness, freedom, autonomy, and strength of will. Consider the lead wolf: he, or the I that is he, roves at will outside the home in which I am still living, just a little boy. Like the dog in London's novel, I progress from a lesser to a greater self in becoming a wolf: I become a big boy. Second, the wolves suggest sexual curiosity—also a way of becoming a big boy, and in more than one way. Consider the dream text as I recall it, which always specifies "*the* bedroom," not "*my* bedroom." The wording casts me in the role of junior Wolf Man: my dream wolves, like those Freud's patient saw sitting candelabra-like on the branches of a tree, are looking with heightened attention (his "strained," mine merely keen) at what must be my parents' bedroom. The image combines a fantasmatic act of looking at a window with the real one of looking at a TV screen. For on all those Saturday mornings when my parents were in bed, I did lead a pack that looked intently at what was forbidden. What the dream wolves are seeking, what their freedom and outcast wildness gives them the power to seek, is the adventure show of sexuality, the primal truth unreeled in the primal scene.

That truth, however, must be forever deferred until "next week." Not knowing what he seeks, the dreamer finds his reward in the breathless excitement of suspense: in the act, not the out-come, of looking intently at the window.

It is hard to imagine this cluster of meanings forming in the psyche of a five-year-old boy, especially given their association with narrative pleasure rather than with fear. For the boy, each element in the cluster must be strictly and frighteningly prohib-ited. So the dream, though it is certainly authentic, must func-tion for me as a device to symbolize and synthesize values and experiences from my later life: it must be a "screen dream" in analogy to what Freud called "screen memories." That would be why I have always remembered it so vividly. The same conclusion is supported by the detail of the rose garden, which is echoed in the "Schubert" dream and runs like a deeply pleasurable leit-motif through my conscious memories of early childhood. The garden is the bedroom, the bedroom is the garden; the garden enclosure even has a windowlike opening on the side facing the house. If the wolves "succeed," they will find a homecoming that does not form the conclusion of an Oedipal story, that cannot be recounted by an Oedipal voiceover.

Reorientations

In "Recollections of the Arabian Nights," Tennyson turns to the legendary east to write an allegory of Western subject-formation, not as it is, but as he would wish it to be. Here is a condensed version, the first stanza coupled with the final three:

> When the breeze of a joyful dawn blew free
> In the silken sail of infancy,
> The tide of time flowed back with me,
>   The forward-flowing tide of time;
> And many a sheeny summer-morn,
> Adown the Tigris I was borne,
> By Bagdat's shrines of fretted gold,
> High-walled gardens green and old;
> True Musselman was I and sworn,
>   For it was in the golden prime
>   Of good Haroun Alraschid.
>
> The forescore windows all alight
> As with the quintessence of flame,

A million tapers flaring bright
From twisted silvers look'd to shame
The hollow-vaulted dark, and stream'd
Upon the mooned domes aloof
In inmost Bagdat, till there seem'd
Hundreds of crescents on the roof
    Of night new-risen, that marvellous time
    To celebrate the golden prime
    Of good Haroun Alraschid.

Then stole I up, and trancedly
Gazed on the Persian girl alone,
Serene with argent-lidded eyes
Amorous, and lashes like to rays
Of darkness, and a brow of pearl
Trimmed with redolent ebony,
In many a dark delicious curl
Flowing beneath her rose-hued zone;
    The sweetest lady of the time,
    Well-worthy of the golden prime
    Of good Haroun Alraschid.

Six columns, three on either side,
Pure silver, underpropt a rich
Throne of the massive ore, from which
Down-droop'd, in many a floating fold,
Engarlanded and diaper'd
With inwrought flowers, a cloth of gold.
Thereon, his deep eye laughter-stirr'd
With merriment of kingly pride,
    Sole star of all that place and time,
    I saw him—in his golden prime,
    THE GOOD HAROUN ALRASCHID.

The poem is explicitly devoted to what Freud called "the family romance." The term refers to an ideal narrative, originally the product of fantasy, that combines two wishful principles. The first is that one's childhood was composed of a self-sufficient trinity of gratified self, gratifying mother, and beneficent father. The second is that one's desires, although limitless, fit snugly into the container of that trinity. The family romance was never more seductive than it is in this text. Here is an Oedipal story with an anti-Oedipal happy ending. The speaker, the ego in the time of its apprenticeship, wanders through a multitude of canals and pathways, maternal spaces shaped under paternal law, and finds nothing but pleasure at every turn. In the labyrinth of this fabled "inmost Bagdat," it is impossible to get lost. Every wrong step takes one closer to home. And "home" is above all the presence of the beautiful mother, in whom all desire concentrates, on view with the kind consent of the beaming father.

Furthermore, this "inmost Bagdat," the child-self's oriental utopia, is not only "recollected" by the poem but also recreated by it. Although what the poem describes is officially the fantasy life that the speaker led in the past, the result of the description is to carry past fantasies into the present. The retrospective mood of the poem suggests that the speaker is recollecting pleasures that he can no longer experience, but the poem's narrative and imagery suggest that he is actually constructing in the present much of what he thinks he recollects. Nonetheless, the main work of recreation does not occur at the level of narrative or imagery. The poem is disarmingly candid about its own fancifulness and does not ask the reader to enter naively into its overt fantasy. Rather, the fantasy becomes covertly available in the sensuous and sonorous texture of the verse, the combination of rich orotundity with a lulling, repetitive, "arabesque" rhythm. These purely performative features give the poetic voice a material richness, a hypnotic physical presence, that gives pleasure in excess of the poem's quaint, nostalgically distanced overt content. The pleasure that the subject has had to surrender in the course of its formation can be recovered in the materiality of this poetic voice, with which both the subject and the reader can freely identify.

Technically, this voice puts the pleasure it offers in the service of a higher value. The voice speaks for the symbolic order; its goal is the revelation of the ideal father, ruler, and lawgiver. But the voice continually exceeds itself. Like the scene it describes, it is enchanted; like the speaker it represents, it is dizzy with its own labyrinthine movement. This voice speaks for the symbolic order only by submerging the solidity of symbolic truth in the ambiguous fluidity of what Julia Kristeva calls the semiotic: the rhythmic, "musical," presymbolic articulation of primary drives (29, 40–43). Inmost Bagdat appears like something seen under rippling water, or in flashes amid the spirals of vertigo.

In the mesmerism of those spirals, the covert anti-Oedipal fantasy nestles. Tennyson's speaker discovers an Oedipal triangle unburdened by rivalry, jealously, hostility, or fear of castration. (Only the sheer length of the poem's meandering, the many stanzas intervening between the ones quoted here, betray a sense of strain in the fantasy, lightly marking the missing elements as more repressed than surmounted.) Discovering the amorous Persian girl in the royal household, the speaker mimics Haroun Alraschid's desire for her, but without looking over his shoulder; he has no dread of reprisal. His desire both enjoys and relinquishes the girl in the same gesture. Although he gazes at her alone, undisturbed and happy, his gaze and all its pleasures freely confirm her as the proper beloved of the other, older man, the man of whose "golden prime" she is "well worthy." She is desirable precisely insofar as she desires Haroun's desire and attracts his gaze. Yet this confirmation robs the speaker of no pleasure, spurs him to no resentment.

In turn, the speaker woos the ultimate favor, the love of Haroun Alraschid himself, by mimicking the desirability of the Persian girl. Not only does the speaker's own eye see Haroun, but it also sees Haroun's own eye, the deep and "laughter-stirr'd" eye that sees one as one wants to be seen. The speaker's eye captures Haroun's gaze. In so doing it lays claim to its own subjectivity.

At his journey's end, therefore, the speaker gains bliss by a primary act of gender synergy. He first identifies with Haroun Alraschid's position toward "the sweetest lady of the time," and then identifies with the lady's position toward Haroun. Superficially, this final position is the Oedipally correct one, with the male aspirant in a feminine relation to a man in his golden prime. But Haroun Alraschid himself is also in a "feminine" position: one that paradoxically, and quite un-Oedipally, defines his unimpeachable paternal masculinity. Haroun is a passive superego figure who rules without judging or prohibiting and who, enforcing no absolute virility, produces no desire for it in others. Haroun is the superego of gender synergy; the Persian girl is his double, his alter superego, as well as his beloved. When the speaker crosses the threshold between these two figures, he becomes the conduit for the *jouissance* figured in the million shooting lights of the city, lights scattering bliss as if they were scintillating orgasmically across the dark of the eye.

Aria

Whitman's favorite music was serious Italian opera, the "electric, pensive, turbulent, artificial" theater of sexual violence, the nineteenth-century equivalent of music video in its devotion to gender polarity. Opera, says Catherine Clément, is the undoing of women made beautiful, the anointing of the soprano as a dying swan. Whitman agrees, but he likes to see tenors die, too. He is artlessly candid about the fact that his love for this particular art bespeaks a taste for eroticized suffering. Nothing in the world is as beautiful as this death.

Yet Whitman manages to make even this music the medium of gender synergy. In the central section of "Proud Music of the Storm," he traces the history of his musical taste. In so doing, he also traces his passage from childhood to manhood, from the imaginary order of narcissistic pleasure to the symbolic order of law and desire, from fusion with the mother to separation from her:

Ah from a little child,
Thou knowest soul how to me all sounds became music,
My mother's voice in lullaby or hymn,
(The voice, O tender voices, memory's loving voices,
Last miracle of all, O dearest mother's, sister's, voices;)
The rain, the growing corn, the breeze among the long-
    leaved corn,
The measur'd sea-surf beating on the sand,
The twittering bird, the hawk's sharp scream,
The wild-fowl's notes at night as flying low migrating north
    or south,
The psalm in the country church or mid the clustering trees,
    the open-air camp meeting,
The fiddler in the tavern, the glee, the long-strung sailor
    song,
The lowing cattle, bleating sheep, the crowing cock at dawn.

All songs of current lands come sounding round me . . . and
    oe'r the rest,
Italia's peerless compositions.

ll. 59–71, 74–75

The fluid, overlapping, association-rich images in this passage enact a gradual metamorphosis of the musical alpha, the sound of the mother's voice in the baby's ear, to the musical omega, "Italia's peerless compositions." At the furthest remove from the hypnotic, otherwordly embrace of "[the] mother's voice in lullaby and hymn," restless this-worldly voices resound in operas by Verdi, Donizetti, and Bellini: voices, most of them, caught up in same sexual economy of (dis)possession, (in)fidelity, and violence that finds its narrative voice in Tolstoy's Pozdnyshev:

Across the stage with pallor on her face, yet lurid passion,
Stalks Norma brandishing the dagger in her hand.

I see poor crazed Lucia's eyes' unnatural gleam,
Her hair falls back loose and dishevel'd.

I see where Ernani walking the bridal garden,
Amid the scent of night-roses, radiant, holding his bride by
    the hand,
Hears the infernal call, the death pledge of the horn.
. . . .
By old and heavy convent walls a wailing song,
Song of lost love, the torch of youth and love quench'd in
    despair,
Song of the dying swan, Fernando's heart is breaking.
"Proud Music" ll. 76–83, 87–89

Bellini's Norma brandishes a dagger against the lover who has
betrayed her; Donizetti's Lucia uses a dagger on the husband
forced upon her. Verdi's Ernani, pledged to commit suicide when
his new wife's old fiancé blows a horn, hears his death-pledge in
the garden of sexual love; Donizetti's Fernando, in despair because his beloved wife was formerly the king's mistress, presci-
ently recognizes the garden of sexual love as a death-pledge. Being an erotic chameleon, and, so to speak, an aesthetic Minotaur,
Whitman finds equal value in the sacrifice of young women and
young men. Opera lets him become both the dagger and the
body that sheathes it, both a Pozdnyshev without guilt and Pozdnyshev's wife without harm. He thereby anticipates Clément's
position with a queer twist. The sexual violence of opera does not

require the undoing of a woman as such, but rather of whatever person is invested with the greatest charge of desire.

All of which comes over Whitman as sheerest bliss. He becomes a virile listener precisely where the lurid gender polarities of the operas collapse most extravagantly into bel canto song. The dirge of polarity and the dithyramb of synergy become one and the same. This ecstatic union occurs, it erupts, when sexual violence charges the air, a lightning bolt in the making. The text marks the union by further uniting the virile pleasures of spectatorship with the blind rhythmic pleasure, the "feminine" pleasure, of the receptive ear. On the one hand are the stage vignettes etched sharply for the gaze, the exquisite visual detail of Lucia's hair and Norma's face, the visible, "radiant" scent of roses in Ernani's garden. On the other hand is the pulsing influx and reflux of the "wailing song, / Song of lost love, the torch of youth and life quench'd in despair, / Song of the dying swan."

Then, just at the point where the identity of eye and ear, masculine and feminine, polarity and synergy, is strongest, the journey that winds endlessly away from the mother reveals that its goal is the mother as well. The musico-autobiography closes with a passage, curiously enough a passage in parenthesis, in which the mother returns in the figure—which is to say both the trope and the person—of Whitman's favorite singer, the prima donna Marietta Alboni:

(The teeming lady comes,
The lustrious orb, Venus contralto, the blooming mother,
Sister of loftiest gods, Alboni's self I hear.)

ll. 92–94

With the appearance of Alboni, bel canto song itself becomes a personified light received into the ear. The portmanteau word "lustrious" crystallizes this effect, turning the illustriousness of the famous singer into the lustrousness of her maternal presence, and that, in turn, into the ritual of lustration by which the listener-spectator is purified. Similarly, the phrase "Venus contralto" identifies "Alboni's self" with her voice, while the enraptured fluidity of Whitman's syntax further identifies that voice-self with a "lustrious orb." Alboni's self, her full-bodied voice, and the orb—orb of her mouth in song, orb of the moon, orb of the breast—become one. Caressed or embraced by the strange parenthesis, the mother is retranscribed from a vague pre-Oedipal substance, irrecoverably lost behind gender polarity, to a precise, everpresent anti-Oedipal synergy of Venus and Diana, the sea-born goddess and the goddess of the lunar orb, the oceanic voice of sexual love and the heavenly voice of chastity and childbirth.

Gensynderergy

The figure of gender synergy intends to evoke a vibrant hetero-
geneity, a patching and piecing of things together into a whole
that is never a unity. It is always a dynamic figure; it stresses the
hand, not the eye; it projects, not the sense of looking at a synergy,
but the feel of making one. It is synergy in motion, like film montage or hypertext, but it is material, palpable in a way montage and
hypertext are not. Gender synergy is more like musical improvisation. Perhaps there is even something intrinsically musical
about it, something that (if we believe their texts) Tolstoy dreaded
and Whitman desired. That would be why, confronted with real
music, Tolstoy listened vengefully, with anger and suspicion,
while Whitman listened gratefully, with endless self-abandon.
Considering this musicality, we could just as well speak of gender
jamming: jamming the machineries of gender, jamming the transmitted images of gender, and all through the kind of improvisation
practiced by jazz musicians who get together impromptu—used
to do, anyway—for the sheer hellacious pleasure of it. If *jouissance*
can get you into a jam, a jam can get you into *jouissance*.

Le Baton ivre

Probably the most familiar of phallic objects, so common as to be almost invisible, is a stick: any of the myriad forms of stick—ruler, scepter, pointer, switch, wand, thyrsus, staff—that simultaneously serves a practical function and makes a symbolic statement. Call the general form of this stick the rod: at once the traditional symbol of authority, discipline, and punishment, and a simple tool for measuring, pointing, upholding, divining, and beating.

The rod is the familiar appendage of the master, who alone is entitled to bear and to wield it. It embodies the coalescence of virility, truth, and violence, as Hector Berlioz once recognized by metaphorically identifying the symphony conductor's baton with both a tomahawk and, by double entendre, the penis. A woman or novice who picks up the rod is taken for ridiculous or dangerous. The sorcerer's apprentice of legend is harried by a pestle (not the pedestrian broom of later versions) that he is helpless to control. The shrew threatens with a raised index finger, the dominatrix with the butt end of a whip.

The rod is also the implicit referent of the typographical mark known technically as the virgule, a term deriving from the Latin *virgula*, which means "little rod." Also known by the ominous name of the slash, the virgule is the mark that articulates polarities: either/or, true/false, masculine/feminine. One way to describe the problem addressed in this book is to say that the purely conventional use of the virgule to form the couple *masculine/feminine* actually conceals and rationalizes a long regime of sexual violence, while at the same time the apparently wrongful infliction of sexual violence actually serves to uphold a purely conventional order.

Yet even the rod is subject to gender synergy. In "The Thyrsus," a prose poem celebrating the music of Liszt, Baudelaire interprets the archaic symbol of the thyrsus as the embodiment of genius. He explains that the thyrsus per se is a simple rod or stick, which is adorned by a garland of flowers. In essence it is a virile form. When he describes the thyrsus in detail, however, the floral adornments prove to be just as essential as the rod. They are not really adornments at all, but essential feminine forms that must be present in order for the masculine form to show itself:

> Never did a nymph, driven to frenzy by the invincible Bacchus, shake her thyrsus over the heads of her maddened companions with such energy and wantonness as you[, Liszt,] your genius over the hearts of your brothers. The rod is your will, steady, straight, and firm, and the flowers, the wanderings of your fancy around your will, the feminine element executing its bewitching pirouettes around the male. Straight line and arabesque . . . all-powerful and indivisible amalgam of genius, what analyst would have the detestable courage to divide and separate you? (72–73)

To some degree, this passage trades on a nineteenth-century cliché that defines the genius as a man whose rich humanity embraces a feminine aspect.[15] There is no parallel category for women. But the passage also disrupts this cliché; written in praise of intoxication, it is intoxicated by gender delirium.

To begin with, the "feminine element" does not subordinate itself to the masculine rod, but instead initiates a wandering and dancing movement that has no clear boundaries. This "arabesque" movement takes the rod as a center, but not necessarily as a rule or curb. Next, Baudelaire warns against reseparating the masculine and feminine elements that are fused in the "amalgam of genius"; the analyst who did so, presumably a man, would render the manly virtue of courage "detestable." What is more, Liszt's genius in particular shows itself by emulating a feminine model, that of a Bacchante, whose (feminine) wantonness he equals along with her (masculine) energy. Finally, the figure of the Bacchante renders the question of the original gender of genius permanently moot. The Bacchante acts on behalf of a male god, but that god, Bacchus, is the most sexually ambiguous in the Greek pantheon, a languid, effeminate figure from whom there nonetheless emanates an "invincible" destructive power, and who, incidentally, was born twice: once from the womb of his immolated mother, and once from the thigh of his father, Zeus.

Perhaps the most hopeful thing about this passage is the way its routine polarization of the phallus and the flower gradually turns into something else entirely, something dizzy and unexpected. Officially, "The Thyrsus" is not "about" masculinity and femininity at all. The topic, rather, is the indissoluble mixture of will and spontaneity that characterizes the greatest art. "What imprudent mortal," Baudelaire asks earlier in the text, "would dare to say whether the flowers and the vines have been made for the stick, or whether the stick is not a pretext for displaying the beauty of the vines and the flowers?" This imagery, however, refuses to signify nothing but art. Like the vines and the flowers, it exfoliates into a "mysterious fandango" of sexual desires and identities that exceed the rule of the "heiratic rod." Baudelaire did not go looking for gender synergy in this text, and he did not find it. It found him.

Lifelines

It sometimes proves convenient to tether men as well as women to positions of abject femininity. Even men who don't act the part may be conscripted, along with those who do, to bear femininity as a stigma in order to ratify the masculinity of other men.

Nineteenth-century Europe and America witnessed a progressive feminization of the role of the creative artist.[16] Together with the parallel figure of the gay aesthete, the modern stereotype of the sissy—maybe gay, maybe not, one could hardly tell and that was the problem—hails from this period. Men whose artistic identities within their chosen field rested squarely on the Oedipal myth of male mastery were nonetheless seen from the outside as holding feminine positions in culture. Sensibility gradually came to rival or exceed formal mastery as the touchstone of artistic character, and a considerable literature linked artistic creativity to the "excessive expansion of nervous matter—great sensibility—acute sensitiveness—quickness of apprehension" (Winslow) thought to be typical of "mental disease" in general and the preeminently feminine disease, hysteria, in particular.

If male artists were to claim cultural authority, they would either have to repudiate this feminizing trend or revalue it. They could, and many did, reactively identify their vocation with the repression (in all senses) of femininity. But they could also seek to destabilize the Oedipal order in which the feminine is always subject to, but never the subject of, culture. Tennyson's *In Memoriam* (1850) treats the second alternative as nothing less than the fulcrum of modern life.

The poem is an extended elegy for the shining friend of Tennyson's young manhood, Arthur Hallam, who is mourned not only for his own sake but also as a lost incarnation of ideal manhood itself. The poem is also a radical statement of gender synergy, and was received as such under the banner of worry over a homosexuality that could not quite be named.[17] If nothing else, the sheer ardor and tenderness sustained through one hundred and thirty-three elegiac lyrics made it plain to everyone that Tennyson's love for Hallam exceeded all common measure, even in an era that fostered Romantic friendship. At one point, Tennyson even risks comparison between his lyrics and Shakespeare's sonnets, some of which had long been clouded by suspicions of sodomy:

> I loved thee, spirit, and love, nor can
> The soul of Shakespeare love thee more.
> *61*

In Memoriam represents an extreme from which Tennyson himself retreated in the famous conclusion to his parable about feminism and its discontents, *The Princess:*

Yet in the long years liker must they grow;
The man be more of woman, she of man;
He gain in sweetness and in moral height,
Nor lose the wrestling thews that throw the world;
She mental breadth, nor fail in childward care,
Nor lose the childlike in the larger mind.

Canto 7, ll. 263–68[18]

At first glance, this passage seems like a prescription for gender synergy wrapped in a benign version of Darwinian evolution. But the terms of androgynous exchange are not even. The man is told once (i.e., reminded) not to lose the qualities that make him dominant; the woman is told twice (i.e., admonished) not to lose the qualities that make her submissive. The new order of gender reinscribes the basic hierarchical structure of the old.

In contrast, the Tennyson of *In Memoriam* represents a fluid reciprocity of masculine and feminine positions as basic to the love he shared with the living Arthur Hallam. This allows him, as the dead Hallam comes to personify the ideal subject of culture, to represent the ideal subject-position itself as both masculine and feminine in relation to a complementary dependent position. In crude terms, the imaginary referent of the master or donor subject may be either the phallus or the breast—or both at once. It is important to stress, however, that gender complementarity does persist in this system of representations. The dependent or recipient position is always touched by abjection; Tennyson dislocates the Oedipal order, but he does not escape it.

In mourning Arthur Hallam, the Tennyson of *In Memoriam* moves freely around a circuit of family-based subject-positions.

The early phases of the sequence are dominated by this mobility; between lyrics 6 and 20, Tennyson figures himself (directly or by analogy) as Hallam's feminine betrothed (*6*), masculine wooer (*8*), husband (*13*), brother (*9*), and son, the latter with Hallam as both mother (*9*) and father (*20*). The movement from lyric to lyric, accordingly, is imbued with a mercurial, pre-Oedipal impetus that undercuts all Oedipal fixities, fixities conspicuously embedded in the bourgeois family structure that Tennyson utilizes as a theater of positional exchanges. Even at the end, where a Tennyson family wedding might seem to recuperate the Oedipal order, a superior mobility intervenes. Tennyson assumes the paternal subject-position for the occasion, but only fictitiously, because the bride he gives away is his sister. A true subject-position is reserved for Hallam-like members of a future generation who will not receive knowledge from a master's instruction but look upon it "eye to eye" (*130*).

The prototype of all this pre-Oedipal mobility is the amity between Tennyson and Hallam. Though it enshrines what Tennyson takes to be the best traits of Victorian manhood—love of learning, the pursuit of knowledge, paternal kindness, civic-mindedness—this amity is represented as a blessed anachronism, its proper soil the unhistorical and essentially unfamilial ground of Arcadian pastoral:

> [For] each by turns was guide to each,
>> And Fancy light from Fancy caught,
>> And Thought leapt out to wed with Thought
> Ere Thought could wed itself with Speech. . . .

> And many an old philosophy
>> On Argive heights divinely sang,

> And round us all the thickets rang
> To many a flute of Arcady.
>
> 23

Tennyson and Hallam, *Arcades ambo*, unite pleasure and knowledge in a continual exchange of masculine and feminine positions, the figure for which is nuptial.

After Hallam's death, Tennyson transfers this idyllic libidinal economy to the idealization of his friend as a Victorian gentleman (*111*), a conquering yet benign subject of culture whose person stands at the crossroads of knowledge and pleasure. Mobile as ever, this anti-Oedipal subject is represented in extreme and bifurcated terms. One set of figures depicts him as a true phallic hero—and hero of phallic truth: the potent voice and steadfast pillar of public life (*113*), the strong victor over religious doubt (*96*), the master bowman who cleaves the mark of knowledge (*87*), the wise, learned, and remote if loving husband of a simple wife (Tennyson, who here adopts an abject posture of "feminine" masochism) (*97*). Another set of figures, often within the same lyrics, depicts a donor position held by a feminine subject, but one that can only express itself in Hallam's manly form. The action of this subject tends to be signaled by figures of pleasure in Hallam's voice, face, or both; traces of primary oral pleasure in the breast emerge when speech or song is identified or associated with flowing liquid (*87, 89, 109, 116*).

The reciprocity between the figures that Tennyson derives from the phallus and the breast is strikingly illustrated in lyric 87, where Hallam as master bowman (masculine) is instantaneously transformed into Hallam as mellifluous singer (feminine). Recalling collegiate debates on art, politics, and commerce, Tennyson praises Hallam's sure shooting over the "slack" performance of other youths:

> And last the master bowman, he
> > Would cleave the mark. A willing ear
> > We lent him. Who but hung to hear
> The rapt oration flowing free
>
> From point to point, with power and grace
> > And music in the bounds of law?

By means of an almost zany mixed metaphor, the listener's willing ear functions as a displaced form of the target of phallic mastery, perhaps suggesting an earlier displacement from body to target, before it appears as the eager receptacle for the free-flowing stream of oral pleasure.

In Hallam's personification of them, masculinity and femininity become nonhierarchical terms. Tennyson, indeed, hails the feminine subject most explicitly in an apostrophe to Hallam's manhood:

> [A] manhood fused with female grace
> > In such a sort, the child would twine
> > A trustful hand, unask'd, in thine,
> And find his comfort in thy face.

113

As the latent image of mother and child suggests, fusion and intertwining occurs not only within the feminine donor subject but also between that subject and her dependent (masculine) complement, intimating a cultural order that is matrix rather than law, fluid rather than rigid at the boundaries of the ego.

Hallam is most prominently foregrounded as a feminine subject in lyrics 84 and 89. In the former, Tennyson imagines the
life that Hallam might have lived, figuring the realization of his
friend's promise with the traditionally feminine image of the
moon waxing from crescent to full. A domestic scene turns on
Hallam as a maternal presence, "A central warmth diffusing bliss
/ In glance and smile, and clasp and kiss"; once again oral pleasure is allied both to its original medium, fluid and enveloping,
and to the sight of the mother's face. Tennyson, as the dependent
of this maternal subject, names himself the uncle of Hallam's
boys, but his displacement from fatherhood is barely veiled. He
fantasizes calling Hallam's unborn sons his own and invokes the
bridal flower (intended for a sister he can hardly bring himself to
mention) that has already been wished onto Hallam in an earlier
lyric:

> Could we forget the widow'd hour
>> And look on Spirits breathed away,
>> As on a maiden in the day
> When first she wears her orange-flower!
>
> *40*

Although the present lyric goes on to celebrate the cultural work
that Hallam would have done in his masculine aspect, it continues to figure this work from within the feminine sphere of do-
mesticity. Tennyson imagines himself sharing in

> the flowery walk
>> Of letters, genial table-talk
> Or deep dispute, and graceful jest.

Hallam's "prosperous labor" occurs as an offstage parallel to
these household pleasures.

Lyric 89 describes Hallam's visits to the Tennyson family home at Somersby; it recapitulates key elements from the earlier Arcadian, domestic, and collegiate idylls (*23, 84, 87*). Hallam is pictured recumbent on the lawn, reading Tuscan poetry aloud; as in lyrics 84 and 87, his free-flowing musical speech diffuses a primary oral pleasure—"bliss," says Tennyson, adding that "heart and ear were fed / To hear him." Hallam's performance is suggestively paralleled by that of "A guest, or happy sister," who plays on the harp and sings a ballad to the "brightening moon." Even more suggestive is the Arcadian close of the poem, which celebrates the oral pleasures of Hallam's and Tennyson's intimate colloquies:

> We talk'd: the stream beneath us ran,
> The wine-flask lying couch'd in moss. . . .
>
> And brushing ankle-deep in flowers,
> > We heard behind the woodbine veil
> > The milk that bubbled in the pail,
> And buzzings of the honeyed hours.

In this scene, the subject is (s)he who, in speaking, gives milk and honey: the maternal breast; the Biblical promised land; the Platonic intoxication of poetry, drawn from the soul as the Bacchantes draw milk and honey from the rivers;[19] the material embodiment of labor (milking) as pleasure (the bubbling—babbling?—milk).

Tennyson seems to have partly modeled the Somersby idyll on the second half of Coleridge's "Kubla Khan," as if to imbue the domestic scene with visionary as well as pastoral qualities:

> A damsel with a dulcimer
> In a vision once I saw. . . .

> Could I revive within me
>   Her symphony and song,
>   To such a deep delight 'twould win me,
> That with music loud and long,
> I would build that dome in air,
> That sunny dome! those caves of ice!
> And all who heard should see them there,
> And all should cry, beware! beware! . . .
> And close your eyes with holy dread,
> For he on honey-dew hath fed,
> And drunk the milk of paradise.

ll. 37–8, 42–49, 52–54

Both Hallam and the "happy sister" stand in the place of the damsel with the dulcimer, and the sound of milk and honey at the close of Tennyson's lyric recalls Coleridge's closing image of the inspired poet who has fed on honey-dew and "drunk the milk of paradise." But whereas the Coleridge of "Kubla Khan" seeks mastery as a donor subject through the song of the maid but fails to find more than wishful conditionals—"could I . . . I would"— the Tennyson of *In Memoriam* seeks and finds empowerment as a recipient subject in the fluid sound of Hallam's voice. Under the Oedipal regime, empowerment as a recipient is a contradiction in terms. But the Oedipal regime is precisely what Tennyson's text seeks to unsettle.

Unlike its Oedipal counterpart, the ideal subject of culture in *In Memoriam* lacks the will, and perhaps even the power, to accuse. Its moral effect depends not on instilling guilt, but on rousing emulation, attaching pleasure to "the vague desire / That spurs an imitative will" (*110*). Poised between the breast and the phallus, this anti-Oedipal subject addresses itself to, rather than inscribing itself on, its object.

The disciplinary rule of the superego, however, is only mitigated, not abolished, by the emergence of a rival moral configuration within the subject. Peter Sacks has argued persuasively that the resolution of the mourning process in *In Memoriam* leaves an acquiescent Tennyson in the classical position of the Oedipal son, entirely dependent on the love and approval of the internalized father, the superego. Sacks cites lyric 124, in which Tennyson claims that the "blind clamor" of his grief has made him wise because he behaved, through it all, "as a child that cries, / But, crying, knows his father near." "The abandoning and abandoned mother," Sacks writes, "is thus replaced by a father, under whose aegis the poet has apparently unmanned himself, but with consoling effects" (199). Despite my emphasis on the poem's anti-Oedipal impetus, I see no reason to contest this reading. The psychosocial action of *In Memoriam*, as I have emphasized, unfolds within and against, not beyond, the Oedipal order.

Nonetheless, the lyric in which Tennyson's grief conclusively dissolves, and not just in solace but in rapture, rests its claim to authenticity on the animating presence of the doubly gendered, anti-Oedipal subject. Lyric 130, the penultimate poem in the sequence, replicates the key terms of the Somersby idyll (*89*) but expands their scale to encompass the whole of Nature. Hallam is apostrophized:

> Thy voice is on the rolling air;
> > I hear thee where the waters run;
> > Thou standest in the rising sun,
> And in the setting thou art fair.

What art thou, then? I cannot guess;
> . . . I seem in star and flower
> To feel thee some diffusive power.
. . . .
> I prosper, circled with thy voice;
I shall not lose thee tho' I die.

A materialized, semiliquid voice in motion; real liquid flowing in parallel; a diffusive, bliss-bearing power—the representation of the maternal matrix is lavish. Its terms, however, have been divided to admit the interposition of a masculine figure, an apotheosis of Hallam himself as a potent and beautiful sun god or son god. The masculine and feminine terms, with their supposedly antithetical effects of distance and envelopment, act in unison; the cycle of the rising and setting sun is mirrored in the circle that, writes Tennyson, the omnipresent voice traces around him.

Tennyson's claim to "prosper"—grow rich from his "investment" in mourning, become Prospero-like, at last divide Hesper from Phosphor (see *121*)—is undoubtedly problematical. Its repossession of the lost Hallam is, to say the least, extravagant, and open to the charge of being merely a regressive image of pre-Oedipal bliss, a fantasy bounded by Oedipal stringencies it can do nothing to alter. Tennyson himself suggests a fringe of reservation; his "star and flower" echoes Wordsworth's "She Dwelt among the Untrodden Ways" (1799), where a star and flower belong to the mourning poet's state of mind *before* death has intruded on it:

A Violet by a mossy stone,
> Half-hidden from the Eye!

—Fair, as a star when only one,
   Is shining in the sky!
ll. 4–8

What is important here, however, is not that Tennyson fails
where no one can succeed, but that he is seeking to empower—
has cumulatively sought to empower—an anti-Oedipal discourse
that in turn will empower him. According to Freud, the superego
traces its origin to things heard (*Ego* 42); in Oedipal terms, the
donor subject of culture is he who speaks, the recipient subject
she who listens. Tennyson, too, authorizes a speaking subject,
but one whose flow of speech feeds, like the (imaginary) breast,
the ear and heart of the listener. So fed, the listener may speak as
well; the donor and recipient are he and she, or she and he,
through whom speech circulates.

Fascinatin' Rhythm

Pozdnyshev loathes Trukhachevski at first sight, yet he seemingly can't get enough of the man. He virtually seduces this object of loathing, not only by his own smarmy politesse, but more importantly by making bait of his wife, dangling her before the violinist's roving eye—and hand: virtually pimping for her, as Richard Leppert observes (171). It is as if Pozdnyshev were compelled to make the archetypal Other Man, the phallic one, appear in person, perhaps in order to master him, perhaps in order to woo him. (Leppert notes the strong current of unacknowledged homoeroticism in Pozdnyshev's fascination [169–70]. We might even say that Pozdnyshev asks music to awaken his wife's desire for Trukhachevski in order to keep his own desire dormant.) Trukhachevski is not merely encountered; he is conjured up. "If he hadn't appeared," says Pozdnyshev, "there would have been someone else. If the occasion had not been jealousy it would have been something else" (398).

But the outcome of this conjuration is infuriating. This other man, this archetypal Oedipal rival, bears the phallus only in hiding, as if concealed in his violin case. He is no masterly presence but just a "not-bad-looking" cad; he does not look phallic in the least. In fact he looks just like a woman:

> With moist almond-shaped eyes, red smiling lips, a small waxed moustache, hair done in the latest fashion, and an insipidly pretty face, he was what women call "not bad looking." His figure was weak though not misshapen, and he had a specially developed posterior, like a woman's, or such as the Hottentots are said to have. They too are reported to be musical. (397–98)

Trukhachevski's red lips and bulging bottom suggest that masculine desire, the result of unstinted participation in the sexual marketplace, is in and of itself feminizing within the nineteenth-century bourgeois order. The man who successfully becomes the subject of desire finds himself prompted to identify with the object of desire and thus paradoxically defaces himself as a masculine subject. Worse yet, the character of this identification suggests that masculine desire by its very nature includes the feminine desire to be desired, to relate to the object of desire not as a proprietor but, uncertainly and ambivalently, as both proprietor and property. Hence, on the one hand, Trukhachevski's effort to look attractive, which Pozdnyshev sees as fey primping: the French fashions, the waxed mustaches, the au courant hairdo. Hence, too, on the other hand, Pozdnyshev's impotent fury at these details, combined with his festishistic fascination by them. ("Though I did not realize it, I observed everything connected with him with extraordinary fascination" [405].)

The ultimate medium of this fascination is music, in particular the first movement of the "Kreutzer" Sonata. The music evokes in Pozdnyshev the same combination of desire, identification, and repulsion at both that the sleazy-charming musician does. In this connection it is particularly striking that Pozdnyshev initially fails to recognize the nexus of sexual desire and gender positioning that the Beethoven Presto arouses in him. He makes this recognition only in retrospect, several nights later. Awakening suddenly in the middle of the night, he recalls that, after the Beethoven, his wife and Trukhachevski had played a whole stroke more: a nameless little piece "impassioned to the point of obscenity" (414), presumably something like ordinary sentimental salon music, something that at the time "[made not] a one-hundredth part of the impression the first piece had" (412).

Only through this little extra piece does the element of phallic display in the Beethoven, and its effect of virtual adultery, become manifest. Pozdnyshev's initial misrecognition of that display has been spurred by his unwilling susceptibility to it. The Beethoven has produced in him an unknown, unknowable, but "very joyous" state of mind, replete with "new feelings, new possibilities, of which [he] had till then been unaware" (411). He embraces this new condition with a "feminine" combination of yielding and avidity. In so doing, however, he also builds up a desperate need to reject the music, to expel it, which later appears as an expression of visceral disgust: "Ugh! Ugh! it is a terrible thing, that sonata. And especially that part" (410). What Pozdnyshev hears in the Beethoven, what he has turned procurer in order to hear in it, is a movement of transcendence, a breakthrough into a spirituality quite inconsistent with the lust, décolletage, and triviality of the drawing room. Yet it is only in the drawing room that the breakthrough can occur; the sign of the breakthrough is, precisely, a transfigured drawing room: "All these same people, including my wife and [Trukhachevski,] appeared in a new light" (412). Pozdnyshev's rage and resentment may thus come from his unwelcome understanding that this visionary experience of his can be generated only through the sleazy, illicit medium of music, the medium, above all, of the feminine, the feminized, and the feminizing body. In killing his wife, he is killing that body, above all killing it in himself. Hence, perhaps, a telling later image: dying, his wife lies on his side of the bed.

Mincing Along

Tolstoy hears the second movement of the "Kreutzer" Sonata as a "beautiful, but common and unoriginal, andante with trite variations" (412). But is Beethoven really returning to the salon here? Charles Rosen thinks so; he, too, describes this "beautiful" slow movement as "elegant, brilliant, ornamental, and a little precious," and adds that it belongs to a "totally different style" than the first movement (399). And it is true that the slow movement begins by parading its good behavior, cultivating a genuine but deliberately stilted beauty. It even seems to be seeking a lulling monotony. The theme and first three variations follow the most redundant of classical melodic patterns, the somewhat old-fashioned "rounded binary," A A B A B A, this one drawn out even further by making the B strains eleven bars long rather than the more customary eight. Both strains of the theme are heard first on piano, thereafter on violin, but this modicum of internal dynamism is lost in the variations, where each strain has only a single form, repeated literally. All of this studied formality, however, is scheduled to vaporize in the last variation. Here literal repetition ceases as each strain adds something new in texture and melody; the music dissolves in rapid ornamentation, it assumes a fantastic delicacy and inventiveness, exfoliating into a poignant sense of radiance, of a lost innocence recaptured, in the instruments' bright upper registers. The ensuing coda, long enough to stand in for a fifth variation, is quasi-improvisatory and expressively diverse, suggesting a subjective mobility to which the last variation has found the gateway. These transformations are what Tolstoy cannot hear, and what it is important for him not to hear. For to hear them without the distance supplied by a judicious formalism would be to hear like a Trukhachevski: and what one would hear, and what would draw one fatally, like a Siren song, is pure gender synergy.

The first movement is more "audible" because it is pure gender polarity. Here there is nothing feminine; even the contrast between first and second themes, which is often glossed as a masculine-feminine opposition, can seem brusquely pro forma, the choralelike second theme serving merely as a parenthesis, a voice from outside that highlights, by deferring, a continuation of the first theme and its headlong energy. The movement as a whole is borne on and born of the masculine body, emblematized at the outset by the rich strenuousness of the violin's double stops and propelled dynamically in the main sonata sections by intense, repercussive, muscular melodic figuration. Donald Tovey called this movement "a magnificent piece of Homeric fighting" (68), and rightly so; it belongs to the closed virile world of Achilles and Patroclus, or the equally virile German-Classical world of Winckelmann (ideal grace, the sculptural, the broad, clear sonata form) and Hölderlin (the rhetorical force, the expressive intensity, the uncontainable passion). "Homeric fighting" also suggests what is most admirable about the movement, what keeps its masculine ethos from lapsing into mere gynophobic belligerence. The music is pure gender polarity, but a gender polarity that abstracts and depersonalizes its violence, that uses its formal design to embed this violence, as Homer does by his epic similes, in the wider circle of destinies—mythic for Homer, social for Beethoven.

And then the second movement! That volatizing and transfiguration of ornament in the last variation, that unharried pleasure in the field of the treble, the high voices of both instruments blissfully intertwining but without erotic friction; the erasure of surplus repetition and stilted-static texture in both the variation and the coda, their increasingly "open" forms full of dynamism without pressure—all this is gender synergy, and all, by compulsion, silenced by Tolstoy. Tolstoy could hear, could let himself hear, only convention in this movement, which, unlike the first, offers no refuge from gender trouble.[20] He could be attracted to the Homeric masculinity of the first movement even as he felt it to impose the composer's all-powerful phallic will on him and thus even as he dreaded and abjected this imposition in the person of Trukhachevski. But what could be dreaded or abjected here?

The answer, Beethoven's own answer, was *everything*—the whole second movement, and, for good measure, the whole sonata. For Beethoven, one part of Beethoven, must have felt as Tolstoy did, have decided to hear only convention in his middle movement. That might explain why he followed it with a flashy, even a trashy, piece of virtuoso superficiality, a brilliant tarantella written originally for another piece, thoroughly effective, thoroughly superficial, thoroughly—shall we say?—cynical. By this means he can repress the uncertainties that the second movement retrospectively reveals in the Homeric ethos of the first. As he would also do in the "Appassionata" Sonata, he had written a two-part form, supplanting violence by bliss, that could not stand as such. Convention required a third movement, partly just in order to deny legitimacy to such a two-part design and the possibilities of gender synergy it releases. (Beethoven finally revoked the convention in his final piano sonata, Op. 111.) So Beethoven condemned his own deviancy by writing a swaggering miles gloriosus of a finale. He "corrected" his errant departure from the heroic standard by reinvoking that standard parodistically: in other words, the first time as tragedy, the second as farce.

Unedited Text of the
Second Wolf Dream (ca. 1972)

⸙

The dream is set on an island, which is full of pines, in winter, in a light, persistent snow, at night. There is a woman who wants to leave—I remember only that her reasons are bitter, and involved with others—but who decides, as she goes, to stay, at least the night. I see her (my consciousness present but disembodied) standing, muffled, surrounded by falling snow, at the door of a white, slatted, wooden house. She knocks, and I know she won't get in. She knocks. From my perspective, I see, outside the white wood gate, huddled in a trenchcoat, very dark against the snow, a burly, slouching figure. I know he is waiting for her. When her knocks go unanswered for a time, she turns and walks away into the night, the snow, amid the trees. The man follows. An older woman now comes to a window, peers through a lifted blind, scowls, and disappears. . . . Now the scene shifts. I see (still disembodied) a wide path in the pinewood. The trees are darkly, glowingly green in the moonlight; the snow falls lightly; it is silent—an unearthly silence and a remarkable, calm beauty. In the distance two dark forms lie writhing on the snow. The woman (I knew she would be) has been attacked: I know that. Suddenly, I am looking towards the vantage point from which my eye saw them lying there. I see, moving towards me (and them, though they're behind or below me): I see, I think, a horsecart or carriage lurching shakily but silently through the snow, drawn, I suppose, by horses, and flanked by animals—I don't remember what kind: horses, cattle, deer? Now once again I look at the struggling bodies—now as if I were coming near with the cart, the animals. I see the man and the woman: but *what* I see (what they are) is a pair of large black bears dandling each other on the snow. Now, on the spot they occupy, there is, there comes, a white wolf who displaces them, makes them vanish. He treads lightly on the snow. He is identified with me. The dream seems done. I sleep. . . . —It is all amidst the beauty and the silence, without anguish—strangeness, mainly; my metamorphosis is my only embodiment in the dream: and I can't tell you how strange and how good it is to be a beautiful white wolf treading lightly on the light snow . . .

A Blind Spot

Tennyson can imagine gender synergy from either a masculine or a feminine position, but he can imagine it only in relation to a man: himself as wife, mother, brother, or son; his partner as brother, husband or father. Not that he rejects gender synergy directed towards a woman; the idea simply never occurs to him. This lacuna (this lack where the woman is) suggests that one function of Tennyson's synergies is to contain same-sex desire within an imaginary matrix of cross-sex relationships. As a side effect, cross-sex relationships themselves are immunized from ambiguities of gender.

Femininity is thus the blind spot in Tennyson's construction of subjectivity—or call it a blinding spot, a scintillation that both protects and endangers the observer by hiding an abyss. Although Tennyson's homoeroticism allows him to embrace and revalue a wide range of feminine positions, including the most abject, the results sometimes harbor a residue of hidden violence. Consider lyric 60 of *In Memoriam*, in which Tennyson jumps class-position—for proper Victorians an even more formidable barrier than gender—to masquerade as "some poor girl whose heart is set / On one whose rank exceeds her own." The longing of the girl, whose love makes her excruciatingly aware of "the baseness of her lot," symbolizes both the longing of Tennyson on earth for Hallam in heaven and, more broadly, the longing of humanity in general for a "nobler" estate than can be found in this world, the "dark house where she [the girl] was born." By wholeheartedly identifying with her unconditional feminine pathos, Tennyson ennobles the abject girl. But by taking her abjection up into a complex chain of metaphors and weaving it into the complex turnings of his verse, Tennyson also enhances that abjection. Nobility carries the girl up only as far as abjection casts her down. The abjection can be enhanced without limit precisely because it has become an instrument of nobility.

Masculine abjection, in contrast, always debases; it disfigures; it castrates. In "Tithonus," Tennyson imagines a monologue by the Greek lover of the goddess of dawn, who asked her for eternal life but forgot to ask for eternal youth. Abjectly feminine in relation to the goddess, a passive, clinging, dependent, figure of pathos, Tithonus swings, pendulum-like, between reliving long-lost *jouissance* in the morning light and vainly longing for death. He has become the repugnant residue of his own lost masculinity:

> [T]hy strong Hours indignant work'd their wills.
> And beat me down and marr'd and wasted me,
> And tho' they could not end me, left me maimed . . .
> And all I was in ashes.
>
> *ll. 18–20, 23*

How can thy nature longer mix with mine?
Coldly thy rosy shadows bathe me, cold
Are all thy lights, and cold my wrinkled feet
Upon thy glimmering thresholds.

ll. 66–69

A shape sculpted in ash, Tithonus waits for the touch or the breath—only the lightest is needed—that will scatter him, and, by his absence, restore his dignity. But masculine abjection is sculpted in granite. Tithonus is still waiting.

Love Knots

Freud says that erotic love must unite two separate currents of feeling, the tender and the passionate. Whitman keeps the two separate, directing his tender feeling toward men, his passionate feeling toward women. His representations of same-sex desire accordingly tend to produce gender synergy, whereas his representations of cross-sex desire tend to fall back on gender polarity. Fortunately, Whitman is not really comfortable with polarity, and his versions of it often seem ready to collapse into synergy at the slightest provocation. Yet there is, even so, an important asymmetry here. Although one might want Whitman to allow same-sex desire to declare its eroticism more openly, it is hard to argue with tenderness:

> Publish my name and hang up my picture as that of the
>   tenderest lover,
> The friend the lover's portrait, of whom his friend his lover
>   was fondest,

Who was not proud of his songs but of the measureless ocean
  of love within him, and freely pour'd it forth.
                                        "Recorders Ages Hence" ll. 3–5

The phallic order of culture, however, requires that a man's passion for a woman take shape as a kind of violence, ideally as a
violence curbed and sublimated, but as violence nonetheless. And
so, in a poet otherwise so remote from endorsing violence of any
kind, it too often does:

O to be yielded to you whoever you are, and you to be
  yielded to me in defiance of the world!
O to return to Paradise! O bashful and feminine!
O to draw you to me, to plant on you for the first time the
  lips of a determined man.
                              "One Hour to Madness and Joy" ll. 7–9

I pour the stuff to start sons and daughters fit for these states,
  I press with slow rude muscle,
I brace myself effectually, I listen to no entreaties,
I dare not withdraw till I deposit what has so long
  accumulated within me.
                                   "A Woman Waits for Me" ll. 27–29

Passages like these can seem clumsy and oddly conventional, as
if Whitman felt masculine swagger as more of a duty than a pleasure. It is only when passion insinuates violence into same-sex
desire that he is fully engaged.

For Whitman knows, even if he knows-without-knowing, that
this same violence operates on men. Here is a series of vignettes
from the original, 1855 version of "The Sleepers," a poem in

which the speaker enters the sleep of a host of strangers, passing lightly through some, lingering with others, in each case identifying himself with the sleeper's dreams and desires:

> I am she who adorned herself and folded her hair expectantly,
> My truant lover has come and it is dark.

⁊⊗⁊

> Darkness you are gentler than my lover. . . . his flesh was
>   sweaty and panting,
> I feel the hot moisture yet that he left me.

⁊⊗⁊

> Be careful, darkness. . . . already, what was it touched me?
> I thought my lover had gone. . . . else darkness and he are
>   one,
> I hear the heart-beat. . . . I follow . . I fade away.
>
> O hotcheeked and blushing! O foolish hectic!
> O for pity's sake, no one must see me now!. . . . my clothes
>   were stolen while I was abed,
> Now I am thrust forth, where shall I run?
>
> Pier that I dimly saw last night when I looked from the
>   windows,
> Pier from out the main, let me catch myself with you and
>   stay. . . . I will not chafe you,
> I feel ashamed to go naked about the world,
> And am curious to know where my feet stand. . . . and what is
>   this flooding me, childhood or manhood, and what crosses
>   the bridge between.

⁊⊗⁊

> I see a beautiful gigantic swimmer swimming naked through
>   the eddies of the sea

What are you doing you ruffianly red-trickled waves?
Will you kill the courageous giant? Will you kill him in the
    prime of his middle age?
Steady and long he struggles;
He is baffled and banged and bruised. . . . he holds out while
    his strength holds out,
The slapping eddies are spotted with his blood. . . . they bear
    him away. . . . they roll him and swing him and turn him:
His beautiful body is borne in the circling eddies. . . . it is
    continually bruised on the rocks,
Swiftly and out of sight is borne the brave corpse.

                                       ll. 46–47, 53–54, 57–67, 81, 85–90;
                                           all ellipses are Whitman's

The sequence of scenes passes from focused heterosexuality to diffuse homosexuality and from confused lovemaking to a welter of solitary desperation, mutilation, and death. As the verses progress from the woman in love, through the denuded man at the pier, to the naked, vulnerable swimmer, there is a steady rise in eroticized cruelty and violence. (There is also a complex interlude, omitted here, that passes from recovered confidence in masculine sexuality, through the vigil of a "sleepless widow," to the reverie of a body—the husband's body?—in its coffin.)

The woman in bed, unobserved, suffers a rough and sweaty friction that leaves her bewildered and unsatisfied. The man at the pier is the object of a classic scene of hostile observation— the defining function of the superego; lost in the dark as the woman is, he writhes with shame at the desires he exposes helplessly with every motion, every word. The pier itself measures his shortfall; it stands like a phallic totem to which the lost man clings, distracted with humiliation, a castrated figure in a frenzy of penis-envy. When the swimmer appears, lost in the nocturnal waters, the mind's eye that observes him is no longer hostile; rather it is fascinated, driven by a voyeurism that piously declares itself involuntary even as it battens on every detail of the swimmer's destruction. To the extent that what amounts to the swimmer's rape-murder by the "ruffianly" waves invokes and satisfies the observer's own desires, to the extent that the whirlpool that sucks in the "beautiful giant" is the vortex of those desires, Whitman comes face to face here with a sexual violence stripped of its pretext in femininity, a violence that precedes any and all of its objects.

The Pobble That Has No Toes

Tolstoy's wife-murderer frets about doing the deed in his stocking feet. The omission of shoes renders him undignified, somehow unmanly: in the world of gender polarity, any absence can become a castration.

In this case the missing item is both a fetish, a nice firm extension of the body to replace the absent phallus, and a bit of body armor, a safeguard for a tender part; Pozdnyshev's wife has, after all, stepped on his toes. On the one hand, or rather foot, the man's shoe capitalizes on the value of a more popular fetish, the woman's shoe, while sidestepping the debasement that the woman's shoe imposes. On the other, the shoe identifies comfort and protection with the tread of the solid middle-class householder, the sort of man who does not parade (or sneak) around in his socks and who could hardly be missing the phallus in the first place.

No wonder, then, that Pozdnyshev cannot feel quite right about killing his wife without wearing his shoes. But on the reading just given, the shoe-logic, already cobbled together for two left feet, continues to trip over itself. In the first place, if Pozdnyshev could wear his shoes he would have no need to kill his wife. In the second place, the absence of his shoes means that he *must* kill her. In the third place, the murder, given this absence, will not be quite satisfactory. A murderer in his stocking feet is not really a murderer, even though his victim is really dead.

Hence Pozdnyshev, as always sharing the fate of Coleridge's Ancient Mariner and the glittering eyes that betoken it, is compelled to tell his story over again to strangers—presumably neither for the first time nor the last. As it happens, his murderous intention crystallized on a train journey, so the story of his crime must be narrated—over and over?—on a train journey. Each renarration constitutes an attempt to get the murder right; but it always goes wrong. Sexual violence always "comes short" of its goal, reinscribes the castration it spectacularly denies, requires its own repetition at another time, in another place, on another woman's body.

Becoming Disowned

The subject of gender synergy takes pleasure in a decentered "self," pleasure in the self's decentering. But what is this famous center, the loss of which, dreaded or celebrated, is supposed to be a cardinal fact of our postmodern condition? One way to think of the center is as what Freud called the ego ideal, the imaginary person one wishes to be. The pleasure of self-esteem is the pleasure of fusion with this person. In Oedipal culture that fusion would coincide with the perfect unbroken articulation of gender polarity. By contrast the pleasure of gender synergy would consist in the practical everyday deconstruction of the ego ideal, its continual unveiling as a cluster of many, perhaps innumerable persons one wishes to be—sometimes. The pleasure of self-esteem would be the pleasure of circulating among these persons, including the deconstructed one.

The self that enjoyed such pleasure would, or could, be something more than the private, patriarchal, hegemonically oppressive creature that forms the familiar target of radical critique. The subject of synergy provides the site where the polarities that underwrite such critique, especially polarities of public and private, outer and inner, are abrogated, their boundaries blurred and allowed to overlap. And this is important: this is necessary. Without pleasure in the self—without narcissism—neither identity nor altruism is possible.

The Politest Castration

Whitman's well-known poem "As I Pass'd through a Populous City" harbors a secret:

> Once I pass'd through a populous city imprinting my brain for
>   future use with its shows, architecture, customs, traditions,
> Yet now of all that city I remember only a woman I casually
>   met there who detain'd me for love of me,
> Day by day and night by night we were together—all else has
>   long been forgotten by me,
> I remember I say only that woman who passionately clung to
>   me,
> Again we wander, we love, we separate again,
> Again she holds me by the hand, I must not go,
> I see her close beside me with silent lips sad and tremulous.

The secret is pretty obvious, hidden in plain sight in the "glass closet":[21] in its original version the poem was about a man. Should we be conventional and assume that the revision was meant to conceal same-sex romance behind a cross-sex pretense? That might do for someone else, but Whitman's poetry in general does not hide same-sex romance; it parades it. So something else must be at work. Isn't the problem rather that Whitman abandons his beloved, that he makes the beloved vulnerable, clinging, trembling, tearful? That's a woman's role: the beloved plays Dido in drag to Whitman's Aeneas. By revising from "he" to "she," Whitman avoids placing his male beloved in the feminine position a second time, and disavows having done it the first time: better that the beloved should be a woman from the outset. Even though Whitman never has qualms about exposing a feminine position of his own, he is careful not to expose another man's. His revision is primarily protective of the beloved, not of himself. He is being polite.

A Sight for Sore Eyes

"Have you ever seen a naked woman?" asks a man who can't stand the view in August Strindberg's play *Creditors*. "Yes, of course! A youngster with developed breasts, an unfinished man, a child who has shot up and then stopped its growth, a chronic anemic who loses blood regularly thirteen times every year? What can anyone like that amount to?" (158).

This statement, backed by the best medical science of 1888, the year it was written, plays out a basic theme of feminist psychoanalysis. In men's eyes women embody a lack of being, symbolized by the anatomical "lack" of a penis. The man who recognizes this supposed castration must recognize, too, that it could also happen to him, if it hasn't happened already. Strindberg's character confesses as much by the excessiveness of his disgust. His response to the female body, or rather to the traumatic memory of it, is plainly hysterical, especially in relation to the thought of blood. Such hysteria is itself a "feminine" quality—though not one usually found in women. In order to avert it, the

fatal lack in women's bodies is typically rendered invisible by giving men something to see. The eye is distracted by adornments,
veils, props, poses, fabrics, cosmetics, tricks of the light, tricks
with hair, anything that conceals as much as it reveals. It does not
matter whether this process works by glamorizing or degrading
a woman, by fetishizing or objectifying her: the woman's lack is
veiled by making her an eyeful. Whatever the means, she re-
stores, even becomes, the phallus of which she threatens the
absence.

I have no doubt that this scenario is played out all the time.
But is it really the whole story (a phallic question)? Isn't the very
uncertainty of phallic authority, real enough at one level, at another level just a pose? a confidence trick? It is a strange sort of
weakness that fuels so much real domination by men over
women. It is a strange form of anxiety that grounds a system of
visual pleasure in which so many men and women constantly par-
ticipate. Perhaps castration is less the fatal flaw of masculinity
than the secret key to male success.

The logic of gender polarity is inflexible. Someone must always be castrated: which is to say, someone *else*. The man in an
economy of lack needs women to embody that lack. If the spectacle of the feminine drapes a veil over the lack, it does so only to
prepare for the moment when a masculine hand strips that veil
away. To see the lack is not to confess vulnerability: seeing the
lack in someone else and making others see it in themselves are
among the defining privileges of the absolutely masculine position. In myth, they are the privileges of Perseus, who not only
saw the Medusa harmlessly mirrored in his shield but also stole
the single eye shared among her protectress-sisters the Graiae.
Perseus's shield, adorned with the Medusa's severed head, be-

comes the frame for the other's lack as trophy. The stolen eye makes its former sharers see that all are blind. Since, however, there is no Perseus outside of myth, no real holder of the absolutely masculine position, the true story is a little different.

Men forge fictions of feminine lack as the basis on which to spin the fiction of the phallus. The lack is the formal ground against which the phallus appears as a figure. Only when a man becomes disenchanted with it does a woman's lack become threatening. Pozdnyshev, so he tells us, fell in love not with his wife but with a tight-fitting sweater; he designed the woman a moral character to match but still could not respect himself in the morning. Another discontented husband, the protagonist of Chekhov's famous story "The Lady with the Pet Dog," is more easygoing:

> It seemed to [Gurov] that he had been sufficiently tutored by bitter experience to call [women] what he pleased, and yet he could not have lived without [what he called] "the inferior race" for two days together. In the company of men he was bored and ill at ease, he was chilly and uncommunicative with them; but when he was among women he felt free, and knew what to speak to them about and how to comport himself; and even to be silent with them was no strain on him. (413)

Gurov experiences himself as a surplus when confronted with feminine lack; even his silence with women is a kind of surplus speech. He feels himself lacking only in the presence of other men.

Woman, the fiction of feminine lack, serves to protect men from the embarrassment of each other's presence. She hands each man his own facsimile of the shield of Perseus, so good a reproduction it almost seems authentic. Whatever women may do, Woman must be placed in positions where her lack will show.

The only problem is that women are not Woman. If a particular woman balks at her assignment, the man who requires it feels justified in forcing her—hand. But good girls are forced, too, as abused women know. Since women must display lack on Woman's behalf, the mere absence of that display can seem to mandate it. Sexual violence may seem—has often seemed—a good way to implant it. And this violence may take shape, in imagination or reality, in representation or on the body, as the purest, most artistic, most spontaneous of inspirations. The young Tennyson imagined an ethereal beauty of Arthurian romance, a maiden who weaves into a tapestry the sights of a world she is permitted to see only through a magic mirror. He called her the Lady of Shalott. Phonetically speaking, she differs from Sir Lancelot, the man who decides her fate, by the lack of a lance. Lancelot destroys her, accidentally to be sure, just by flashing (Tennyson's word, take it as you like) his reflection in her magic mirror and singing "tirra-lirra." Later on the lady-killer gets to speak her epitaph:

> He said, "She has a lovely face;
> God in his mercy lend her grace,
> The Lady of Shalott."
> *ll. 169–71*

Fullness of being as figure claims the right to arise at any time against lack of being as ground. If Woman is lack, then both Beauty and Truth demand that they fill that lack. But they have to find it first.

"In the far south"

In the far south the sun of autumn is passing
Like Walt Whitman walking along a ruddy shore.
He is singing and chanting the things that are part of him,
The worlds that were and will be, death and day.
Nothing is final, he chants. No man shall see the end.
His beard is of fire and his staff is a leaping flame.

Wallace Stevens,
"Like Decorations in a Nigger Cemetery" ll. 1–6

This figure of heroic masculinity, compounded of the semisy-
nonymous powers to defy limits and to utter prophetic visions,
arises against the half-forgotten scrim of the ocean, the feminine
element that the masculine creative principle, like the sun, illu-
minates but does not touch. The ruddy singer walks on the ruddy
shore as on a boundary line. Men set and cross boundaries;
woman dissolve them. Men observe the line drawn between the

sea and the shore; women, like the ocean, draw that line only in
the act of dissolving it.

In "As I Ebb'd with the Ocean of Life," the real Walt Whitman does something better than his solar namesake. He imagines
himself as a mere scattering of debris cast up on either side of the
wavering line that bounds the shore by the "fierce old mother,"
the ocean:

> Me and mine, loose windrows, little corpses,
> Froth, snowy white, and bubbles,
> (See, from my dead lips the ooze exuding at last,
> See the prismatic colors glistening and rolling.)
> Tufts of straw, sands, fragments . . .
> Up just as much out of fathomless workings fermented and
> thrown,
> A limp blossom or two, torn, just as much over waves
> floating, drifted at random.
>
> *ll. 57–61, 65–66*

The limpness and tearing of the blossoms scarcely require com-
mentary. What inscribes this passage with Whitman's signature
is the tranquillity, the gentle, self-sustaining rhythm, with which
the spectacle of masculine dissolution appears. The images speak
of polarity, the poetic voice of synergy. The masculine self, an-
nulled, releases prismatic beauty from its unmoving lips.

Perhaps Whitman's favorite activity is bathing in and emerg-
ing from the ocean. He loses the boundaries of his ego in order
to find them, and finds them in order to lose them again; there is
no "having" a self outside this rhythm of self-abandonment:

> You sea! I resign myself to you also—I guess what you mean,
> I behold from the beach your crooked inviting fingers,

I believe you refuse to go back without feeling of me,
We must have a turn together, I undress, hurry me out of the
   sight of the land,
Cushion me soft, rock me in billowy drowse,
Dash me with amorous wet, I can repay you.
                     "Song of Myself" ll. 448–53

The passage eddies between doing and enjoying, blurs the line between acting and receiving action; the "I" who undresses may be
the one who hurries (but may be asking to be hurried), may be the
one who cushions himself (but more likely is asking to be cush-
ioned), could be the one who rocks himself (but is surely asking to
be rocked), and at last is the one who asks the ocean to dash on
him, come on him, but only insofar as he can return the favor.
All this, again, is marked, wetted down, with Whitman's bifold
signature—*W. W.:* in this case the mixture of frenzied, "unmanly" passion, the rhythmic urgency of someone shedding his
clothes like a chrysalis, with the firm, easy confidence in the
power to reciprocate the ocean's gifts: "I can repay you."

Aural Sex

Music spellbindingly performed is the great medium of gender synergy. That is what Tolstoy hated and feared in music, and also what Tennyson and Whitman loved in it. "Under the influence of music," writes Tolstoy as Pozdnyshev, "it seems to me that I feel what I do not really feel, that I understand what I do not understand, that I can do what I cannot do. . . . Music carries me immediately and directly into the mental condition [of the man who] composed it. My soul merges with his and together with him I pass from one condition into another, but why this happens I don't know" (410–11). The more masculine the music—say the first movement of the "Kreutzer" Sonata—the more it arouses the femininity within the listener's masculine position, the more it lifts the constraints on emotional volatility, yieldingness, soul-merger, pleasurable subjection. Whitman, who embraces rather than represses the *jouissance* of this process, compares it all but explicitly to sexual penetration through the (r)ear:

I hear the key'd cornet, it glides quickly in through my ears,
It shakes mad-sweet pangs through my belly and breast.
                                          "Song of Myself" ll. 597–98

If this musical pleasure is transgressive, that is because it is always bifold, shell-like, invaginated. It is always given over to a doubling of itself that ignores conventional orders of value: its pleasures are pangs, and vice versa; its sweetness is madness, and vice versa; its sensory location is an occult fusion between the whorls of the ear and of the anus, traditionally the most disembodied and most bodily of our organs-orifices.

Whitman also hears music as a displaced and heightened form of the incessant, teeming polyphony of the world. As such, it becomes the very substance or principle of an infinitely displaceable subjectivity, of a "self" that is always already synergy:

I hear bravuras of birds, bustle of growing wheat, gossip of
     flames, clack of sticks cooking my meals,
I hear the sound I love, the sound of the human voice,
I hear all sounds running together, combined, fused or
     following,
Sounds of the city and sounds out of the city, sounds of the
     day and night,
Talkative young ones to those that like them, the loud laugh
     of work-people at their meals. . . .

I hear the trained soprano (what work with hers is this?),
The orchestra whirls me wider than Uranus flies,
It wrenches such ardors from me I did not know I possessed
     them.
                                          "Song of Myself" ll. 585–88, 602–4

The origin of this subjective fluidity is the mother of earliest childhood—more concretely, as we learn in "Proud Music of the Storm," it is that mother's singing voice. By yielding to such fluidity, by undoing the repression imposed on it by the regimes of Oedipal culture, the masculine subject is ecstatically decentered. The result in "Proud Music" is a continual rhythmic shuttling between "a language of impregnation that defines [Whitman's] creativity as feminine—what he hears 'fills' and 'inflates' him; he feels it 'bending me powerless, / Entering my lonesome slumber-chamber'—[and] a style of [virile] prophetic declamation that unifies 'man and art with Nature' in a return to 'the far-back days the poets tell, the Paradiso'" (Kramer, *Music* 224).

Tennyson hears much as Whitman does, but in bursts rather than rhythms, his blissful receptivity and power to recall the past coming together in poignant, nostalgic moments of fusion. Transfigured landscapes flicker to life as Tithonus relives his lovemaking with Aurora in "days far off" and as Tennyson in his own voice recalls Arcadian walks with Hallam in *In Memoriam* (22–23) or the scenes of an enchanted childhood of "Recollections of the Arabian Nights." In each case the love-transfigured landscape is associated with a dulcet music in the ripeness of a golden age: the song of Apollo in "Tithonus," "While Ilion like a mist rose into towers"; the flutes of Arcady in *In Memoriam;* the song of the bulbul (nightingale), "ceasing not, mingled, unrepress'd," in "Recollections of the Arabian Nights."

In the receptive ear, willing or unwilling, at the threshold of synergy, music brings to life Jacques Lacan's cryptic formula that the Unconscious is the discourse of the Other. The music identifies the "innermost," most "authentic" feelings of the listener with the feelings of someone else, and reveals that these feelings can be authentic and innermost only and precisely because they are those of someone else. For the listener, the resulting position of derivativeness, of secondariness, corresponds to the repressed feminine position embedded within gender-polarized masculinity. But it also corresponds to a position of absolute pleasure, a site of fullness, identity, and bodily vitality rather than of loss, dissociation, and castration. The music charges (entrusts and electrifies) the listener with the desire of synergy; it carries out, pied-piper-like, a violation or coercion or seduction or suffusion or liberation or *jouissance*.

So performed, so heard, any music can do this, even music saturated with the rhetoric of virility or gender polarity; the power to do it is part of the very definition of musicality.[22] Similarly, any performer may be moved to encapsulate the quickening force of synergy in an openly orgasmic gesture: Nijinksy miming masturbation as Mallarmé's and Debussy's faun, Bernstein shaking from head to toe as he conducts the climax of a Mahler slow movement, Madonna imitating Michael Jackson grabbing at his crotch.[23] But there is also music that means to do this, music that *is* this.

Consider once more the second movement of Beethoven's "Kreutzer" Sonata, music that not only culminates in gender synergy but also dramatizes the emergence of that synergy from gender-polarized femininity: music that takes the gratifications of decorous sentiment as stepping-stones to the high-flying rapture of variation 4 and the prismatic expressivity of the coda. On the way to this transfiguration, the music also insinuates a critique of the gender-polarized first movement. Is the first theme of the latter fiercely insistent? The middle movement parodies this insistence in the pat insistence of its own A sections, heard four times each through variation 3. Does the first movement's first theme aggressively hammer out repeated notes? The middle movement parodies this aggression with punctilious repeated-note figures in variations 1 and 2. Is the first movement's minor mode riddled with turbulence? The *minore* variation 3 is almost languorous. The middle movement becomes transfigurative precisely when it reaches an expressive plane that has no parallel in the movement before. The virile stance of the first movement is thus revealed as rooted in a denial of Oedipal vulnerability (obedience to the rule of the salon, a feminine and feminizing rule) as much as in the affirmation of Homeric fighting strength. In Tolstoyan terms—remember Tolstoy's unwilling allegiance to this movement—the first movement's heroism is revealed in retrospect to be less like that of Achilles than like that of Count Vronsky, Anna Karenina's tin-soldier lover. Such heroism is a false front that never stops looking good but that always somehow betrays itself at second glance.

Counterparts

In Beethoven's sonata, the exaggerated masculinity of the first movement and the exaggerated femininity of the first several variations of the second movement melt away into the radical heteronomy of synergy. Yet for this to happen the extremes must be fully unfolded, and not merely pro forma: they must be arresting, each in its kind, the first movement domineering in its relentless passion, the early variations (even the lyric *minore*) alienating in their frigid beauty. Synergy does not deny the appeal of polarity; it requires this appeal; it transforms it.

Obsequies

Pozdnyshev feels a certain obligation to visit his wife's deathbed. "[I] immediately decided that I must go to her. Probably it is always done, when a husband has killed his wife, as I had—he must certainly go to her" (426). Expecting to personify manly dignity in a scene culled from popular melodrama, and once more remembering his stocking feet, he puts on bedroom slippers as the tokens of bourgeois normality and goes to her. But his wife spoils the scene. She reproaches him and denies him custody of the children and, worse than with her speech, undermines his position with her silence: "Of what was to me the most important matter, her guilt, her faithlessness, she seemed to consider it beneath her to speak" (427).

Worse, perhaps, she forgets to put on her makeup. "What struck me first and most of all," Pozdnyshev tells us, "was her swollen and bruised face, blue on part of the nose and under the eyes. This was the result of the blow with my elbow when she tried to hold me back. There was nothing beautiful about her, but something repulsive" (426–27). The point of sexual violence is to punish the victim for vacating the feminine position that ratifies (that masks the dissimulation of) the aggressor's masculine position and at the same time to return the victim to the place she has vacated. But the results of sexual violence unfit her to occupy that place: she becomes repulsive. The marks of violence (on the body, as here, or in behavior—the wince, the cringe, the will to placate) become alienating to the man who has inflicted them; they render the woman even more problematical than she was before. Such marks act as signs of their victim's deviation, reminders that she has slipped her place, that her place may be slipped at will, and that when she slips out of this place the man must slip into it. At the same time, the marks block the man's sexual desire by depriving it of its object; literally or figuratively, the violated woman defaces this desire instead of embodying it. The marks of sexual violence thus make further violence all but inevitable. This is so regardless of the guilt they may also induce in the man (they even induce guilt in Pozdnyshev). If Pozdnyshev had not killed his wife, he would have battered her again. And again.

Just Married

⟨∞⟩

Pozdnyshev, to put it mildly, is turned off by the sex on his honeymoon. He explains his loathing with a pair of loathsome analogies:

> [It was like a time in Paris] when I went to take in the sights, and, noticing a bearded woman and a fishtailed dog on a sign-board, I entered the show. It turned out to be nothing but a man in a woman's low-necked dress, and a dog done up in walrus skin and swimming in a bathtub. . . .
>
> It was something like what I felt when I learned to smoke—when I felt nauseated and the saliva gathered in my mouth and I swallowed it and pretended that it was very pleasant.
>
> *410; translation slightly modified*

Sex in marriage is something that, when you take it in, either takes *you* in, like a sideshow, or makes you want to get it out, like smoky spittle. Of course it's not supposed to be like that. What could be the problem?

In sex the man is familiarly supposed to "possess" the woman, a possession redoubled in the married man's proprietary right over his wife's body, and this act of possession is supposed to ground and ratify the structure of gender polarity. (These metaphors have gone underground since the nineteenth century, but no one should underestimate their persistence, both covert and overt.) What Pozdnyshev discovers on his honeymoon is that sex is a failure at upholding gender polarity, and, more, that its pleasure consists in this failure. Sex continually subverts the sexual difference it is supposed to confirm. Like music, it makes a man feel what he keeps telling himself he doesn't really feel, meaning rather that he is not supposed to feel it. Pozdnyshev does not enter the show in spite of its freakish attractions, but because of them.

But why just these attractions?

The bearded lady and the cross-dressed man, one and the same, raise one and the same question: phallus, phallus, who's got the phallus? Desiring one's wife is like desiring the bearded lady: well, then, does one desire the lady or the beard, and, if the latter, does that mean one has no beard? Desiring the bearded lady is desiring the cross-dressed man: well, then, is femininity merely a screen for the phallus, and, if so, does that mean one lacks the phallus and desires only to "possess" (but how? and how in a woman?) the man who possesses it?

For those who subscribe to it, the sex mandated by gender polarity is a sideshow monstrosity. Its masculine position is like that of a dog cased in a walrus skin and a bathtub, the phallus lost or absorbed in the dark sheath and wetness of the (gender-polarized) feminine. For the man who insists that sex involve the phallus (as distinguished from his penis), it would be better to hold back the emissions of his body and merely pretend to enjoy himself—but this, or so he thinks, he cannot do: there is no holding back and therefore, or so he thinks, no distance, no space of theatricality, no pretense. Sex, including the pleasure of sex, is always to some degree disgusting for the man whose masculine position is polarized. Such a man mistreats women because they make him want to puke up the femininity he has always had to swallow.

Inside Stories

Feminist psychoanalysis has established an interesting scenario to explain why becoming a man involves learning contempt for women.[24] Men, it is said, are trained to repress their own femininity, the product of early identification with the mother, and to project this femininity onto women, who are then looked down on for bearing it. This scenario, which is surely played out all the time, is a basic type of gender polarity, but it is not, I think, the prototype, not the mechanism of gender polarity as such. For all its prevalence, it remains a local effect. The feminine position within the masculine subject can be disclosed or activated in the absence of any overtly "feminine" traits: Tolstoy's Pozdnyshev is feminized by his socks. And even the most "feminine" traits can be tolerated within a sufficiently dissimulated claim to hold the absolutely masculine position: the old farmer of Whitman's "I Sing the Body Electric" is virtually a breast, but he is none the less a man's man of a patriarch.

To go further, and because I especially wish to prevent misreading on this point, I would not trace sexual violence to men's needs either to avoid being feminized or to deny some preexisting internal femininity. Again, the point is not that the latter phenomena are not real, but that their usages are different. On the one hand, men seeking to avoid what they take to be feminization do not tend to turn violently against women, but agonically against other men. On the other hand, as we will see when Tennyson "cross-voices" himself as a Victorian wife, men troubled by what they take to be a feminine component in themselves do not so much deny it as deploy it in order to confirm the deeper truth of their masculinity.

That deeper truth is the critical point here. Both the idea of avoiding feminization and the idea of reacting against internal(ized) femininity assume the presence of an intact core of preexisting masculinity. These ideas therefore serve gender polarity in both theory and practice. In theory, indeed, they serve gender polarity in the very act of criticizing it. What I am suggesting is that no core of primary masculinity exists except as a position always occupied by someone other than the subject. Femininity is the term for the avowed condition of dependence on internalized authority, whether we call that authority the superego or the symbolic order or the good, the beautiful, and the true. This is the condition of all socialized adults. Women are those who are chosen to personify this condition in the avowed space of social life, so that others, called men, can disavow it. (A reminder, perhaps especially pertinent here: this formula may be disturbed or complicated by relationships to and among sexual and racial minorities.)

Sexual violence is a technique for sustaining the root disavowal of psycho-moral dependency when that disavowal is in

danger of failing. Violence against women does not so much deliver men from feminine abjection as deliver it to them; in the
woman's violated body, in her tears, pleas, screams, useless resistance, the violator finds the image of an abjection to which his
masculinity is superior. Pozdnyshev, for example, describes his
wife, staring at him with her hands shielding her bruised eyes, as
a rat in a trap. The symbolic dimension of such violence is sometimes evident in a certain precision and deliberateness that justifies the use of the word *technique*; Pozdnyshev notes that he aims
at, and hits, a particular spot on his wife's torso that he has se-
lected in advance. The symbolic dimension also helps explain
why, as I noted earlier, the threat of violence may work as well as,
or better than, violence itself. Anything that elicits a sign of abjection can help firm up the sagging disavowal.

When violence occurs, however, it often becomes more
mechanism than technique, a notably mindless brutality. This,
too, happens with Pozdnyshev, who admits to feeling a "need for
destruction" and a "transport of rage" that is lawlike in its law-
lessness: "Fury, too, has its laws." One source of this automatistic
excess in sexual violence may be the absence, in gender polarity,
of any viable alternative to the root disavowal. Virtually the only
available recourse is a perversion, masochism, that according to
Kaja Silverman in *Masculine Subjectivity* acts out the acknowledgment of subjective lack denied by conventional masculinity. The
masochist's abjection is an exaggerated form of the normal self-
abnegation that is unremarkable in women until some woman
refuses it. When someone in a masculine position is pressed to
avow the truth of his psycho-moral dependency, what confronts
him is a void; his position suffers a breach, a trauma. The result
is a positional terror that expresses itself as positional terrorism.

A masculine position, we might conclude, can be occupied nontoxically only if it is occupied as an illusion—not in the sense of a mirage but of a professional magician's trick. It must be occupied in all the ways that that gender polarity prohibits: playfully, ironically, provisionally, fictitiously. The masculine image must be something I both see and see through, like my reflection in a pane of glass.

Arietta

"The Kreutzer Sonata" would make a great opera, a *Carmen* without the exoticism of *Carmen*, without all the excuses to be charmed, bourgeois tragedy in its purest form. In my imaginary musical museum the socks aria and deathbed duet become popular concert excerpts. Meeting in the afterlife, Wagner and Puccini deplore the decline of operatic taste so clearly shown by such popularity, but each secretly enjoys the music.

Laura Mulvey says that sadism demands a story (22), and Catherine Clément that opera demands the undoing of women. In the operas of the core canon, closure equals an imaginary woman's corpse enshrouded by the beauty of a real woman's voice. Opera idealizes sexual violence like a Platonic form and, contrariwise, exalts it transgressively as unspeakable pleasure. (Such pleasure, often identified with *jouissance*, supposedly eludes all forms of representation and regulation. If there is any hope for the Pozdnyshevian art of opera it is that a counter-*jouissance* unforced by such grandiose ambitions undoes all this undoing from within.) So strong is the death mandate that it can sometimes be carried out for no apparent reason. For the cruelest instance, see Wagner's *Parisfal*, where the redeemed Kundry drops dead without a word at the height of the climatic Grail ritual. (Or has Kundry finally figured out that the Grail is a fetish and rejected it for a genuinely higher calling? Does she speak in silence for what Wagner has repressed?)

The Pozdnyshevian Art

Recently I saw a performance of *Madame Butterfly* and found myself (of course) irresistibly moved by the lyrical tragedy of the end. But I also found, almost to my surprise, that Catherine Clément actually understates the problem of this tragedy, which requires far more than the sacrificial undoing of a woman. It requires the woman—really just a girl—to endure a torment drawn out by the music like sweet taffy, a passive, purely pathetic torment devoid of any compensatory dignity, heroism, or transcendental illusion.

Butterfly's showstopping aria, "Un bel di," enacts her doomed attempt to sing herself into the bliss of such an illusion. Divided against itself, the aria is barred from attaining the kind of imaginary autonomy that ruptures the cruel dramatic finalities of Lucia's mad scene or Isolde's transfiguration. Deserted by her American husband, Pinkerton, Butterfly reassures her doubting servant, Suzuki, and thereby herself as well, that he is sure to return "one fine day." Looking out to sea, she foretells his return in vivid detail and invests it with rapturous lyricism. But the lyricism of her song is self-consuming. Initially unbroken, the lyrical vocal impulse aims to transcend the fact of abandonment with the feeling of reunion. The lyrical line, particularly the vocal line, seeks to be autonomous in its imaginary gratification. But this same lyrical line also yields repeatedly to pictorial and dramatic gestures from both the voice and orchestra. Signs of what is lacking in reality must supplement the self-referential lyrical presence meant to transcend the lack; the nonspecific stream of imaginary happiness is puckered, increasingly disfigured, by the mimicry of specific bits and pieces of a narrative of reunion that does not and will not occur. This empty musical miming is redoubled by the gestural miming by which Butterfly accompanies her song. By the end of the aria, her lyricism has become hysterical, in the strict turn-of-the-century sense of constituting the symptom of a thwarted desire, a "strangulated affect." Her closing words, "All this will happen. . . . my faith is unshakable," mean just the opposite of what they say; they project the anguish of a loss already suffered but not yet avowed, and this not only in the strident agitation of the orchestra, but also in the vocal stridency needed to make the words heard above that agitation.

Butterfly's seaward gaze is generally directed at the audience—an audience whose sea of faces necessarily gazes back at her with the poisonous knowledge of Pinkerton's racism and callousness, but an audience who also receives the sensuous-sentimental pleasure of "Un bel di" in a continuous tributary stream. Sadism certainly demands this story. However compassionate it may feel, the audience occupies a sadistic position here—just as Kate Pinkerton does in the final act, when she, the

American wife, gives Butterfly sympathy but still takes her child. Everyone feels sorry for Butterfly, but everyone also consents to the spinning out of her torture into silken veils and long surges of seductive vocal melody, the alchemizing of her anguish into the lush heart-tugging sweetness that only an expertly managed fin-de-siècle orchestra can manage to convey.

And who is being tortured? Butterfly, Cio-Cio-San, is a figure of double, mutually reinforcing difference: a woman whose racial otherness renders her infinitely exploitable, a treasure of the east, and a racial other whose extravagant lyrical suffering renders her infinitely feminine, a pearl of great price. By displacing the evils of European colonialism onto the American ravisher, Pinkerton, Puccini absolves his audience of responsibility for Butterfly's suffering and frees them to find a wealth of eroticized pleasure in it; by making his victimized heroine a racial exotic, Puccini sidesteps the need to place limits on his image of femininity as an unconditional supine masochism.

One way to untangle these strands of racism and misogyny is to regard them as inessential, unfortunate accidents of Puccini's being a "man of his time" that are surmounted by the opera's theatrical and musical power. But willful blindness is not much of a solution to problems of this magnitude. Imaginary monsters disclose real fears. It would be more to the point to see what difference it makes to our pleasure that the opera is violent precisely toward a consummate figure of difference. How and why does the pleasure we are offered take as its necessary condition the imaginary abuse of an adolescent oriental girl—a victim who is, of course, and also as a necessary condition of its first performances, impersonated by a full-grown western woman? Once we know what difference difference makes, we will have the problem or opportunity of reconstructing our pleasure in a way that allows us to keep it, as audiences worldwide obviously want to do.

A new concept with an old name has come to light in recent psychoanalytic theory. This is the phantom, a shameful or unspeakable secret transmitted unconsciously from one generation to the next.[25] Considering the ageless popularity of the phantom of the opera, it may be that there is something intrinsically musical about the psychical phantom, which haunts us like a tune whose words we can't remember, and just as well: the memory would be our undoing. Or would it? Shouldn't it be possible to expose the phantoms of our pleasure, and not just in opera: to break their spell a little, to bring to light all the unspoken, unacknowledged, unsuspected premises of our aesthetic investments, and then to see what remains to (of?) us? There is no avoiding some anxiety over the ensuing cost in disillusionment. But might not the gain in openness and meaningfulness outweigh this? Or even, just possibly, offer an unforeseeable gain in pleasure itself?

Diva

Before the invention of sound recording, music was something seen as much as heard. To do it full justice, we have to take a look: to examine what Richard Leppert calls the sight of sound, where musical meaning often lies unacknowledged. Figure 1 shows Thomas Eakins's painting "The Concert Singer." Look at that dress the singer wears, vibrant, flowing, shimmering. In color it is a rich medley of iridescent pinks that virtually overflows the canvas. In connection with the singer's opened mouth, the lips perhaps still parting, and her exposed throat with its deep hollow, the dress is a materialized form of the song she sings and the pleasure it gives (to her? to the listener?). At the same time, the dress serves as a second skin, revealing that the singer's body is the body of pleasure—though whether her pleasure or the (male) spectator's is uncertain. More his than hers; she looks uneasy, her hands more clenched than folded.

In both figurations, the dress is a fetish, virtually the fetish of fetishes. It fills the eye so dazzlingly that it almost works. (Fe-

Figure 1. Thomas Eakins, *The Concert Singer*. Oil on Canvas.
Courtesy Philadelphia Museum of Art.

tishes, whatever their payoff in pleasure, never work in the long run; they always defer more pleasure than they give.) Here is gender polarity at its most seductive. The social detail and the realistic portrayal of the face veil the image of the singing body, that phantasm of polarity, so that it appears as unveiled truth. (Again the exposed throat: vulnerable, alluring, the locus of the voice.) And in this appearance, we (those addressed, the male spectators) find the illusion of a mastery without violence, without violation. In the awkwardness of the singer, her untidy hair, her self-conscious homeliness, we see—we almost hear—her eagerness to please. In the silence of the singer we hear—we almost see—the voice that would please us. Repository of the bliss she cannot keep, released from that open mouth, this voice-phallus is his who views it. He can even seem to grasp it, running his gaze up along the thyrsus of the conductor's baton that, doubling the painter's brush, is held by an anonymous masculine hand at, or into, the bottom left margin of the image.

And what, then, of the female spectators—those not addressed? Should they overidentify with the image (as beauty, commodity, the object of desire—see Doane), or should they purloin the phallus and gaze like a man? Or, far better, should they find the singer's voice in their own throats? Should they dephallicize this voice, recast its silence as their secret, and carry it off with them? Could they see the reluctant flesh and exposed throat as withholding some small quantum of voice from the tidal pull of the dress, as pulsing to an inaudible rhythm that the painter-conductor's hand cannot quite trace, not quite mark with his beat? Could even a man learn to become this lucky feminine spectator?

An Asymmetry

The phallus is a symbolic object, the Janus-faced signifier (Lacan tells us) of desire and subjectivity on the one hand, and, on the other, of the lack in which desire and subjectivity are grounded. But the phallus stands in a relation of complementarity, not to another object, but to a site or bearing, the feminine position. That position exists in order to display a lack that can be made good: a fillable lack, the lack filled by the phallus, the lack by which the phallus imagines itself to be called into being, whereas (but this is a secret) the summons really goes the other way, the phallus calls the lack into being in order to imagine the lack as a call, a call for help, for closure, for rescue. The phallus calls the lack into being in order to become the phallus.

What happens, then, if the feminine position displays an un-fillable lack? If the position goes vacant, especially if it goes vacant abruptly, then unfillable lack is just what its vacancy signifies: not woman-as-lack but a transcendental lack, *the* transcendental lack, which woman-as-lack screens from view and against which, in so doing, it protects the phallus. The empty position is an abyss, a horror, and worse yet a material one. It figures in representation as a trace, an overflow, in the worst cases as the actual mass of a filthy, viscid, repellent substance. ("Sometimes," says Pozdnyshev, "I watched [my wife] pouring out tea, swinging her leg, lifting her spoon to her mouth, smacking her lips and drawing in some liquid, and I hated her for these things as if they were the worst possible actions" [393].) Someone has to be found to clean up this mess; someone has to do the housework. To veil the unfillable lack, someone (else) must be put in the feminine position without heed for cost or consequence. No sacrifice is too great—for the other.

"Isolde sinks, as if transfigured . . ."

⚬⚬⚬

Pozdnyshev gradually discovers that what he has heard in the first movement of the "Kreutzer" Sonata, as played by his wife and Trukhachevski, is a lovedeath. The lovemaking that he sees through, or in, their playing becomes something terrible, something more than mere adultery, precisely insofar as its association with the music promotes it to a lovedeath, a synchrony of passions in which the performers' normal, social identities disappear, leaving them exhausted and transfigured. "I had never seen my wife as she was that evening[—t]hose shining eyes, that severe, significant expression while she played, and her melting languor and feeble, pathetic, and blissful smile after they had finished" (412).

But why a lovedeath? Why, for that matter, is the lovedeath the nineteenth century's favorite fictional moment? Perhaps it is because, in the lovedeath, the actors die so that the spectator might live. Their death absorbs, and turns to bliss, the guilt that the spectator feels for desiring what they do. The imaginary bodies of the actors are consumed by their bliss but leave the bliss behind, make it available to the spectator who is dying to have it and only now can have it without dying. Only the spectator can both experience and survive the lovedeath. Only the spectator can both "have" *jouissance* like a woman (the imaginary experience) and "know" it like a man (the survival). The spectator is thus thrown out of position, thrown beyond positionality itself, and the throw feels indescribably good. In free fall, the spectator is identified neither with the punitive law that demands the death in love nor the obedient receptivity that welcomes love as death. There is no position from which to experience the lovedeath; in that sense it is not experienced at all: it just is. Hence Pozdnyshev's strange joy at the performance of the "Kreutzer" Sonata, the joy of being and having he knows not what—"'That's how it is—not at all as I used to think and live, but that way'" (411). Hence the enormous melodic sequence, an impassioned phrase rising in two crescendos through the whole gamut of semitones, by which Isolde's transfiguration arches to the climatic peak from which it falls, lingeringly falls, and dies away. Hence the tears, sobs, vertigoes, catches and losses of breath that even today spectators bring to their lovedeaths.

"Softly in Brangäne's arms . . ."

So much for the spectator, but what of the lovers? Or, to be more exact, what of the spectator's experience "as" the lovers rather than as their heir? For the lovers, too, the lovedeath undoes the Oedipal structure of positionality, but not quite as it does for the spectator. It creates a state of mania or delirium in which the ego ideal or the superego is sucked into the ego proper, as if to slake an intolerable thirst. The ego's built-in femininity shatters like a chrysalis. The outcome is necessarily fatal, but just because of that, because death is final and eternal, the delirium need never subside, the mania never yield to depression. In the lovedeath the lovers' ego—there is only one—takes spontaneous, irrevocable, but still imaginary possession of the absolutely masculine position.

This remains true even though the active figure in the lovedeath is almost never a man. Only a woman can freely embody the feminine positionality that the lovedeath shatters; only she can testify that the shattering is the acme of both pleasure and justice. Accordingly, the agent of the lovedeath is either a woman who, like Isolde or Brünnhilde, momentarily revives her dead lover's ego in her own and achieves transfiguration over his body, or a composite being formed of a man and a woman in extremis, like Verdi's Aida and Rhadames—often, like this pair, melted together in opera by an ecstatic duet. (Manrico and Leonora from Verdi's *Il Trovatore* nearly form such a double subject in their farewell duet, but Violetta, in *La Traviata*, cheats Alfredo of a lovedeath, and so unmans him, by acting like some Kundry wannabe and dropping dead on her own, a few steps out of reach, and to wrenching music.)

At the same time, however, the absolute position is lost as well as found in the lovedeath. Without an ego to subdue, without a conditional position to instruct and punish, the absolute position cannot be truly itself. In the lovedeath this position is no longer the mighty thing it was—or was supposed to be; it has become purely non-Oedipal. The lovers are more like the spectator than they seem at first glance. For them, too, the position of the lovedeath is positionless.

My second wolf dream depicts this positionless state. The dream's lovedeath arises in the transformation of the violently writhing couple into the dandling bears who, in turn, are amalgamated into the singular and beautiful figure of the wolf against the snow. At one level, of course, I am that wolf, free and happy. At another, more important level, I am only contained in the wolf along with the violated woman, for it is she, above all, who is set free when the wolf springs forth. I blend with, but am not lost in, both the woman and the purifying element, the snow. But I am also present elsewhere, as a spectator. Kept in the distance, condemned to the gaze, do I feel a non-Oedipal yearning and identify with the wolf who recedes from me, or do I feel Oedipal jealousy, envy, desire mixed with rage as the wolf springs forth?

The lovedeath is radically ambivalent. On the one hand, a sheer negation of the Oedipal regime. On the other hand its perfect ratification. No Oedipalized culture can flourish without the lovedeath.

"*Onto Tristan's body*"

The lovedeath is a representation that represents nothing, a mimesis that imitates nothing, a symbol that symbolizes nothing. There is nothing in the real world to which it corresponds. One of the most radical acknowledgments of this occurs in Whitman's poem "So Long," which identifies the subject's lovedeath with the posthumousness of his text:

> Camerado, this is no book,
> Who touches this touches a man,
> (Is it night? are we here together alone?)
> It is I you hold and who holds you,
> I spring from these pages into your arms—decease calls me
> forth.
>
> O how your fingers drowse me,
> Your breath falls around me like dew, your pulse lulls the
> tympans of my ears,

I feel immerged from head to foot,
Delicious, enough.

ll. 53–61

As an imaginary-symbolic resource, the lovedeath is permanently valuable if permanently dubious. It institutes our resistance to complete inscription within the symbolic order; it is the allowable signifier whose signified is the *jouissance* I cannot have except by immersing myself (immerging myself from head to foot) in the signifier.

But the lovedeath is also the unfulfillable wish par excellence; it can never be carried over into reality. Or rather, whenever it carries over, it miscarries in the form of jealous rage. Lurking behind every lovedeath is a figure to interdict the love: in mythic terms, King Mark of *Tristan und Isolde*, who witnesses Isolde's transfiguration; in realistic narrative, a jealous husband, a Pozdnyshev. In my second wolf dream, more figures of jealousy: the woman who lurks behind the door, the rapist who disappears. Jealousy can even create the lovedeath, summon it into being as a tragic destiny: like the murder of Desdemona on the marriage bed, the murder of Pozdnyshev's wife with a Moorish dagger is also a lovedeath. Says Pozdnyshev, taking note of the realities behind the love triangle he has cultivated so carefully: "I saw that from their first encounter her eyes were particularly bright and, probably as a result of my jealousy, it seemed as if an electric current had been established between them" (402–3). And, as the story shows, when the lovedeath carries over into reality the love part divides from the death part: my love, your death.

Chop Logic

Sexual violence is a form of unreason, but it does obey a logic, a rigid logic, a logic of rigidity.

From classical times to the later eighteenth century, Western culture acknowledged a certain ambiguity about the boundaries between masculinity and femininity and policed them with a corresponding latitude. In that era, the indeterminate position all men must occupy was embodied by the figure of the androgynous youth. Whether beardless boy or breastless girl, the youth was familiar as the very archetype of the Desirable. The figure is best known today from Shakespeare's comedies *Twelfth Night* and *As You Like It*, in which the male leads fall in love with girls cross-dressed as youths, who were played on the Elizabethan stage by youths cross-dressed as girls. After the 1760s, thanks to the influential, erotically engaged art-historical work of Johann Winckelmann, the androgynous figure was associated primarily with classical Greek sculpture of adolescent males; the result was both to secure and strictly limit the figure's continuing cultural value, which would become increasingly minoritized and aestheticized during the nineteenth century.[26] By the fin-de-siècle, the same figure has become threatening, dubious, corrupt, often metamorphosing to become the erotic child or perverse old man, like the Tadzio and Aschenbach of Thomas Mann's *Death in Venice*. In all its avatars, however, the youth is primarily the object, not the subject, of desire. (Not-to-desire was the very role of the youth in the institution of Greek pederasty that inflames Aschenbach's imagination.[27]) It is as if desire could spring only from a fixed gender position, the very fixity of which renders it susceptible to the charms of a roving one. And the subject who desires the youth is almost always masculine. His desire, which necessarily marks him as other than the youth, acts as the very mechanism and evidence of the subject's masculinity.

But no man is ever that subject. The man who "is" so always misrecognizes himself. His position is always implicitly that of the youth he desires—desires to have, but never (again) to be. His desire itself may involve misrecognition, and not only because the gender of its object is ambiguous; the subject may interpret his attraction to the youth as erotic in order to mask the fact that it is narcissistic, an idealizing desire to be the youth after all, the cynosure of the desiring eye. To know these things lucidly is itself a kind of castration, and so not-knowing becomes something one holds on to, like a lucky piece, a kind of thought-fetish. Any identification as boy, girl, woman, or epicene provokes a furious denial.

Shakespeare's Coriolanus is the archetype of the disguised boy as charismatic killer, epitomized in the figure of his own small son "mammocking" a butterfly—tearing it apart with his teeth. Coriolanus's mother has sought to secure his manhood by sending him to war "when [his] youth with comeliness plucked all gaze his way" (I.iii.7), but the result is only a domineering effigy. Taunted as a "boy of tears," the hardened soldier proves the point by the sputtering bravado of his response:

> Measureless liar, thou hast made my heart
> Too great for what contains it. Boy? O slave! . . .
> Cut me to pieces, Volsces. Men and lads,
> Stain all your edges on me. Boy! False hound! . . .
> Alone I [conquered]. Boy?
>
> *V.vi.101–2, 110–12, 115*

It can hardly be accidental that the insulted hero's ranting (here much abbreviated) turns on images of size and mutilation. Perhaps it is not accidental either that similar images surface in Beethoven's portrait of the same hero; in the recapitulation of the *Coriolan* Overture, the indignant music that begins the exposition is set askew and scaled down as if to fit an angry boy.[28]

The logic of sexual violence rears up amid these intrinsic confusions of the masculine subject-position. To move (or stay moved) from psychical androgyny to psychical virility, a man must engage in a symbolic performance. He must take conspicuous possession of the phallus he is already supposed to have. (His penis, in this scenario, does him no good at all.) He must adduce a sign, the whole stroke more, *n* to *m*, n(ought) to m(an). Without the sign he is dead as a subject, an outcome often represented by narrative catastrophe: Shakespeare's Coriolanus really cut to pieces, the musical motive of Beethoven's fading away in lank phrases and gaping silences. Violence against women erupts when a woman interferes with the requisite display: prevents the man from grasping the phallus, declines to recognize it in his grasp, refuses to hand it to him (as if it were hers? where did she get it? who is she working for?).

At that point the phallus is to be repossessed at any cost—to the woman. Pozdnyshev seizes it in the form of a virgin dagger, a bridegroom dagger that will stage his impromptu divorce as a wedding night: "a curved Damascus dagger that had never been used and was very sharp" (421). The damask steel, hand wrought, identifies the dagger as a hero's weapon; the same damask steel, steel with wavy lines etched like script along its grain, identifies the dagger-phallus as a kind of writing implement. These identifications converge on the blood evidence that anchored our first encounter with the Pozdnyshev case. With his steel pen the subject inscribes his authority, his identity, on the body of the woman from whom, as from the virgin bride, his implement justly and publicly draws blood.

Even Whitman cannot resist posing, uncharacteristically, with the repossessed phallus. He throws his whole body into it:

> It is I, you women, I make my way,
> I am stern, acrid, large, undissuadable, but I love you,
> I do not hurt you any more than is necessary for you.
> *"A Woman Waits for Me" ll. 25–27*

And doesn't my second wolf dream try to wish the logic of sexual violence away by transforming the two dark figures on the snow, figures whose wrestling already confuses rape and lovemaking, into a single, free, and beautiful white wolf? One wolf, not the Wolf Man's six or seven: a wolf free of the violence of all primal scenes?

But dreams are easy: their wishes are precisely the ones that can't come true. The logic is in place, everywhere. Interference with the repossession of the phallus does not even have to happen in order to trigger real or symbolic violence. Merely the suspicion of it is enough. Displaced or symbolic forms of it are enough, even when, especially when, neither the man nor the woman recognizes them consciously.

—Odd, isn't it (or is it?), but normative violence between men is not played for these stakes. The winner-loser relationship that emerges from male agonics is a structure of social exchange. It is even a commerce in pleasure when the violence is ritual rather than real. The good loser always gets back the phallus he has lost. He gets, you might say, a mortgage on it.

Tall Tales

In traditional narrative, women seek men, but men seek manhood. Traditional narrative is so preoccupied with this search that manhood itself seems to be won as much—or more—in narrative as in reality. Unless a man has a story to tell about his attainment of manhood, he has not in fact attained it. And even if he has a story, it has to be told more than once. The story itself is another one of those little extra pieces by which masculine identity contrives the illusion of wholeness.

Cogito E_go Sum

In one sense gender itself is an extra piece: the phallus of subjectivity. As self, ego, consciousness, the subject is defined by a call to differ from two others, one imperfect but attractive, one harassing but perfect. The bind is that difference from either figure entails likeness to its alternative. This contradiction is projected into social space by identifying its two pairs of adjacent positions (greater Other to self, self to lesser other) with the difference between masculinity and femininity. Why gender should be the chosen medium is not certain. Perhaps because gender is supposed to regulate sexuality, and can therefore form a bridge between sexuality and subjectivity? But the need for this bridge is illusory: there is no gap to be bridged here.

Cavatina

One reason why Whitman loved opera, and in particular serious bel canto opera, more than any other art form is that it constituted a perfect home for his sexuality, which otherwise had none. As Whitman heard and saw them (both processes are essential), the operas of Bellini, Donizetti, and Verdi constituted an eroticized zone, space, or scene, merely to enter which gratified desires that could otherwise not even be named—desires, in particular, for masochistic enjoyment with a woman and for anal penetration by a man. This is from *Leaves of Grass:*

> I hear the violoncello ('tis the young man's heart's complaint),
> I hear the key'd cornet, it glides quickly in through my ears,
> It shakes mad-sweet pangs through my belly and breast.
>
> I hear the chorus, it is a grand opera,
> Ah this indeed is music—this suits me.
> A tenor large and fresh as the creation fills me.
> The orbic flex of his mouth is pouring and filling me full.

I hear the train'd soprano (what work with hers is this?)
The orchestra whirls me wider than Uranus flies,
It wrenches such ardors from me I did not know I possessed
  them,
It sails me, I dab with bare feet, they are lick'd by the indolent
  waves,
I am cut by bitter and angry hail, I lose my breath,
Steep'd amid honey'd morphine, my windpipe throttled in
  fakes of death.

ll. 596–608

The eroticism of this passage, utterly clear and keen at every point, emerges from a logic of displacement or, to speak in rhetorical terms, of metonymy. To find out what is happening at any given site, one asks what is happening adjacent to that site; strands of identity will knot the sites together. This process pulsates under the skin of Whitman's poetry generally, but it particularly tends to surface—to become clear and keen—when sexual desire, especially homosexual desire, is its driving force.

In this case, the young man's heart finds its complaining voice on the cello, the sound of which elides into the keyed cornet; this key, a little extra piece, gives the sound of the cornet the phallic power to glide in through Whitman's ears—the gliding implying an openness, a full lubrication, in the orifice. Since both singer and listener are male, that orifice must be the anus, an identification confirmed by the path of the mad-sweet pangs that shake through the listener's belly and breast. At this point the scene of sexual consummation declares itself to be (or to have become) grand opera. The young man previously heard only in transcription, on cello and cornet, now sings in his own person as the tenor, phallically engorged to be large and fresh as the creation.

It is now the tenor who, through the orbic flex of his mouth, his phallic song, is filling the listener up.

It might seem that nothing could follow this surge of bliss, but now another wave of pleasure succeeds, this time gliding from the tenor to the soprano. Joining with the orchestra (resplitting the voice into human and instrumental sounds) the soprano traces another orb, whirling the listener on the furthest track of the classical solar system and wrenching new ardors from him that take the form of wounding and suffocation (the cutting hail, the throttled windpipe). The result is a lovedeath, the listener's lovedeath, a dose of honeyed morphine that winds him abjectly in coils ("fakes") of musical rope that knot into a simulation ("fake") of death itself.

Nothing in this passage suggests that its erotic adventures are merely metaphorical, or metaphorical in any sense. Opera does not gratify Whitman's desires substitutively, but metamorphically. To be caught up by the opera *is* to find bliss in pain and humiliation, to drown in the honey of the breast; it is to be blissfully penetrated, and that not by a mere penis, but by that for which the penis itself can only substitute, the phallus.

Both the complexity of these pleasures and their reciprocal orientations toward soprano and tenor, mother and comrade, indicate that Whitman's operatic sexuality is a hub, a hubbub, of gender synergy. The main source of this synergy is the peculiar combination of masochism and passive anality (labels that, of course, do not apply for long). In classic masochism, as described by Sacher-Masoch, only a masculine subject can receive masochistic pleasure from a woman. But by the logic of the phallus in Western culture, only a feminine subject can receive bliss in sheathing, rather than wielding, the phallus. Whitman's operatic sexuality allows him to float or surge from one position to the other, to become his own circulation between the "homosexual" bliss of penetration and the "heterosexual" bliss of abjection. My scare quotes acknowledge what may already be obvious: that the lack of boundaries between pleasures and positions collapses the polarity of masculine and feminine and along with it the polarity of heterosexual and homosexual. What sense does it make to say that the listening subject must be either masculine or feminine when it can so easily be both, and perhaps neither? Reborn in opera, the subject is a pure song that has escaped its singer: an aesthetic-libidinal column or stream that pulses from the orb by which one body is opened and glides into the orifices that rescue another body from being closed.

Pleiades

I had read Freud's case history of the Wolf Man a year or so before dreaming my second wolf dream. One reaction, which my dream at once recalled, was regret that the Wolf Man's terror of his father (*homo lupus homini*, man a wolf to man) had blinded him to the extraordinary beauty of his dream: in which, as I imagined it, the winter-fruit of the motionless wolves gradually began to abstract themselves and glitter (the Wolf Man's associations included a Christmas tree) like stars, like a constellation: more, since what the Wolf Man *did* see, however remotely, was a sexual act, to become a star map of the body's pleasures at eyes, ears, mouth, nipples, anus, genitals. My dream inscribed this in the moonlit glowing pines amid the snow, the climactic frolic of the beautifully white wolf.

Clef Change

Childhood sexual experience always seems to have a traumatic edge to it, however pleasurable it may be, and even if it is not marred by abuse from adults—what Freud called "seduction" in order to denote a destructive, illicit sexual initiation. One reason for this is suggested by Jean Laplanche, who proposes the existence of a "primal seduction," an event of childhood that is neither a sexual fantasy nor an experience of abuse but the discovery of an open secret: the first sexual symbol, the first "innocent" word or image that simultaneously veils and unveils a sexual meaning (*New Foundations* 89–164). Laplanche's concept ties childhood sexuality to the permeation of language, or more broadly of representation, by desire. Unlike both the ambivalent fantasy and abusive reality of sexual contact with an adult, which may or may not befall anyone's childhood, the primal seduction would be unavoidable, as would its manifold repercussions and repetitions.

This necessity, however, raises its own set of problems. Is it also necessary that this seduction mark one's subjection to the violence of paternal law by which sexuality is governed? Is the discovery of sexual meaning necessarily a trauma that dispossesses one of the phallus that one has never had and can never have? Or is it possible to take the primal seduction as the threshold of a region of wonders, the semiotic possibilities of which scintillate on all sides like the body's star-points in my fantasmatic reaction to the Wolf Man's dream?

Epiphany

The neurologist Oliver Sacks sees the effects of migraine in the visions of the twelfth-century mystic and composer Hildegard of Bingen—sees them, not to debunk the visions as symptoms, but the reverse:

> Great rapturous intensity invests the experience of these [luminous] auras, especially on the rare occasions when a second scotoma [visual occlusion] follows in the wake of the original scintillation:
>
>> The light which I see is not located, but yet is more brilliant than the sun, nor can I examine its height, length, or breadth, and I name it "the cloud of the living light." And as sun, moon, and stars are reflected in water, so the writings, sayings, virtues and works of men shine in it before me. . . .
>>
>> Sometimes I behold within this light another light which I name "the Living Light itself". . . . And when I look upon it every sadness and pain vanishes from my

memory, so that I am again as a simple maid and not as an old woman.

Invested with this sense of ecstasy, burning with profound theological and philosophical significance, Hildegard's visions. . . . provide a unique example of the manner in which a physiological event, banal, hateful, or meaningless to the vast majority of people, can become, in a privileged consciousness, the substrate of a supreme ecstatic inspiration. (169)

When lights dazzle but are not physically there, we can either accept the bliss of seeing the light that blinds us or, like Hildegard, seek to see *through* our blindness—not only, that is, to see beyond the blindness, but also to see by means of it. Like Hildegard, too, we can understand that the dazzle attends the body as well as the spirit. Objects of desire sometimes strike us metaphorically as radiant, too bright to see, veiled by their own brilliance—the cloud of living light. At other times these same objects throw light in our eyes like a handful of sand so that we stumble in darkness, as when some primal seduction or primal scene brings us face to face with the substance of "a physiological event, banal, hateful, or meaningless."

One way to answer that darkness is to repress it, which is what we do when we see nothing but the light in our eyes—when we see our blindness. But what if we choose to see through that blindness? Hildegard's concentric lights, the scintillating scotoma of classical hysteria that breaks the visual field with a ball of rotating light, the shooting lights in Tennyson's garden of Haroun Alraschid, the incandescent star-point wolves of my fantasy, perhaps the flaming whirlpools of light in Van Gogh's *Starry*

Night: what if all these were to become not so much the work of *re*pression as of *ex*pression, not a refusal to see but a (re)casting of the primal scene, the primal seduction, as a venue of wonder? That would be to imagine a primal scene without violence, without a wound and a weapon, without a phallus. Would it be *jouissance?* or something better?

Conundrum

If sexual violence is really the outcome of a double bind built into normal subjectivity, why isn't it even more prevalent than it is? Here are four answers. One: A critical distance is always potentially available between persons and subject-positions; men are sexually violent for psychosocial, not hormonal, reasons, and may resist sexual violence for the same sorts of reasons.[29] But two: the question is misleading; even men who don't perform sexual violence can "understand" it well enough and may enjoy it in fantasy; the social consequences of this capability are substantial. Nonetheless three: the superego, nasty though it is, is reasonably efficient; it polices the violence it serves to encourage; it makes a man stop short. But four: maybe its lapses into inefficiency should be encouraged. Under the regime of polarity, we are encouraged to talk as if the superego were indomitable, as efficient a top cop as you could ask for. But what if this cop's armor had chinks in it? What if it were possible to live in its gaps, see in its blind spots, above all to enjoy without its approval? What if we could sometimes fool this old cyclops by inhabiting the places that only two eyes can see?

Minstrels

How about a riddle? This one is a bit of Americana. It comes verbatim from *Christy and Wood's New Song Book*, a compilation of songs and jokes from the repertoire of the famous blackface troupe, the Christy Minstrels, published in Philadelphia in 1854: "Why is a man that's taking a popular medicine like a man that's whipping his wife? because he takes an' *he licks her* (elixir)" (Lott 196).

In its original setting, this joke was told by blackface performers for the amusement of an audience consisting mainly of white working-class men. The point of the joke is to resolve a sexual tension in racial terms, and at the same time to resolve a racial tension in sexual terms. By laughing at the joke, the men in the audience can gain access to two kinds of pleasure that would ordinarily be inhibited if not quite forbidden. First, they can enjoy their own hostility to women by displacing it onto a racial other. Second, they can identify with the racial other's mockery of social regulation on the basis of a shared hostility to women. The image of whipping neatly equates the woman with the slave, so that the imaginary act of wife beating endows the audience members with a double sense of privilege, racial and sexual, which is supposed to belong to them but that their actual workaday life may do little to support. In that sense the equation of sexual violence with medicine is a sound home truth: wife beating is the cure for besieged manhood.

An even deeper truth, though, may lodge in the wordplay of this admittedly stupid joke. If we allow submerged meanings to surface, the use of the phrase "licks her" to denote a beating takes on an oral dimension because of its conjunction with the image of taking a liquid medicine. The beating is identified with drinking something restorative, an elixir, an act that in turn is identified with licking a woman. But what every nineteenth-century man once "licked" on a woman to nurture himself, to nurse himself, was a breast. The punning rhetorical equivalence of whipping and licking identifies sexual violence with getting the sweet, the milk, the precious elixir of life. The deep truth of the joke is that such violence is itself a kind of minstrel performance gone wild: not blackface, but babyface.

Tableau vivant

In the last section of "I Sing the Body Electric," Whitman composes an anatomical diagram out of an inventory, a long litany, of body parts, investing a libidinal charge into each and every part, including those considered remote from standard erogenous interest: "All attitudes, all the shapeliness, all the belongings of my or your body or of any one's body, male or female" (l. 147) from sexual organs to the "thin red jellies within." The body's electricity is its sexual magnetism, and vice versa: a new version of Faraday's law.

But it seems as if the human body will, as in Leonardo da Vinci's famous drawing of Man as microcosm, be gender-specific: the body of Man is a man's body. This virile bias overrides Whitman's attempts to generalize; although his inventory announces itself as representing man, woman, youth, and child, the implicit visual scheme is clearly masculine. Surveying the body from head to heel, it duly notes the "manly beard" and chest hair and cen-

ters on the "man-root [and] man-balls." The body is indeed in
the first instance Whitman's own, and its specificity inhibits its
generalization to "your or any one's body, male or female." But
then there is a dramatic shift: a turn, so to speak, on the heel.
With a sudden plunge into the visceral interior, so far unmen-
tioned, the inventory reverses course and reconstructs the body
as feminine, at the same time replacing the single traversal from
top to bottom with a series of rhythmic swings between top and
bottom and inside and outside:

> The lung-sponges, the stomach-sac, the bowels sweet and
>   clean,
> The brain in its folds inside the skull-frame,
> Sympathies, heart-valves, palate-vales, sexuality, maternity,
> Womanhood, and all that is a woman, and the man that
>   comes from woman,
> The womb, the teats, nipples, breast-milk, tears, laughter,
>   weeping, love-looks, love-perturbations and risings,
> The voice, articulation, language, whispering, shouting aloud,
> Food, drink, pulse, digestion, sweat, sleep, waking,
>   swimming,
> Poise on the hips, leaping, reclining, embracing, arm-curving
>   and tightening,
> The continual changes of the flex of the mouth, and around
>   the eye,
> The skin, the sunburnt shade, freckles, hair,
> The curious sympathy one feels when feeling with the hand
>   the naked meat of the body,
> The circling rivers of the breath, and breathing of it in and
>   out,

The beauty of the waist, and thence of the hips, and
downward toward the knees.

ll. 148–60

Masculine structure and singularity is flipped over into its traditional complement, feminine diffusion and multiplicity. The
result of this asymmetrical inversion, however, is not a single
androgynous body. Rather the human body now confounds vi-
sualization. It cannot be drawn as such; it is *not* more than the
sum of its parts. The fully-inventoried, fully-sung body is a palimpsest, or else a shimmering figure variably evoked by the
overlaying of anatomical transparencies on one another. Or perhaps the body is no longer visual at all. As soon as the inventory
has touched on "all that is a woman," it goes on to invoke speech,
as if the Word were born of woman and the fully synergized
body were a body of words. Here is Lacan's symbolic "impos-
sibly" flushed with *jouissance!* Or, to change the figure, the sem-
iarticulated plenitude of body parts ultimately forms a Rabelai-
sian catalogue-aria, a "grotesque" and joyous arglebargle of the
kind imagined by Mikhail Bakhtin: anatomy as festivity, rude
jubilation, carnival.

Passing

The course of Whitman's strange, trancelike inventory of the body can also read as tracing a swing from the pleasures of masculine self-identification to those of an all but explicit transsexual wish: the "wish to be woman."[30] The same wish surfaces in other nineteenth-century men of note, but in most cases with a stern, pre-Freudian proviso: the wish to be woman implies a wish for castration. In his Tahitian diary, Paul Gauguin records feeling a sudden desire "to be for a moment the weaker being who loves and obeys" (57). Daniel Paul Schreber, jurist, memoirist, and paranoiac, records awakening one morning and thinking, while still in bed, that "it really must be rather pleasant to be a woman succumbing to intercourse" (63). He goes on to describe in exhaustive detail the long course of his subsequent "emasculation," his painful-blissful transformation into a woman, by "the rays of God."

Whitman's wish may seek gender synergy, but the more typical wishes of Gaugin and Schreber do not. In their cases, the wish to be woman seeks to uphold gender polarity from the passive rather than the active position. A similar instance, but a much more unstable one, occurs in Tennyson's *In Memoriam*. As we saw earlier, this encyclopedic work traces a grand synergy-like circuit of subject-positions among which "pure" femininity could count only as one position among many. This one position, however, can become so fantasmatically powerful as to threaten a short circuit. Here is lyric 97, complete:

> My love has talk'd with rocks and trees;
>> He finds on misty mountain-ground
>> His own vast shadow glory-crown'd;
> He sees himself in all he sees.
>
> Two partners of a married life—
>> I look'd on these and thought of thee
>> In vastness and in mystery,
> And of my spirit as of a wife.
>
> These two—they dwelt with eye on eye,
>> Their hearts of old have beat in tune,
>> Their meetings made December June,
> Their every parting was to die.
>
> Their love has never past away;
>> The days she never can forget
>> Are earnest that he loves her yet,
> Whate'er the faithless people say.
>
> Her life is lone, she sits apart;
>> He loves her yet, she will not weep,
>> Tho' rapt in matters dark and deep
> He seems to slight her simple heart.

He thrids the labyrinth of the mind,
  He reads the secret of the star,
  He seems so near and yet so far,
He looks so cold; she thinks him kind.

She keeps the gift of years before,
  A wither'd violet is her bliss;
  She knows not what his greatness is,
For that, for all, she loves him more.

For him she plays, to him she sings
  Of early faith and plighted vows;
  She knows but matters of the house,
And he, he knows a thousand things.

Her faith is fixt and cannot move,
  She darkly feels him great and wise,
  She dwells on him with faithful eyes,
"I cannot understand; I love."

It is important to stress that this poem, so distasteful by modern standards, does not voice a fantasy of having an abjectly submissive wife, but a fantasy of being one. Yet the fantasy does not really concern femininity at all, except in an instrumental sense; instead, it arises from and refers to the subject-position of non-absolute masculinity, a position that it seeks, abjectly enough, to idealize.

Tennyson justifies his own ignorance and inadequacy, his limitations as a man, his disqualifications for the role of bard, sage, or cultural hero, by transferring these unmanly qualities to the figure of himself as a woman. He finds his alter ego in the ideal Victorian wife, guardian of an early love her husband has surmounted, a figure loyal, unintellectual, worshipful, and masochistic. In her the poet's defects become graces, even if they are graces to which her husband can only condescend. The cool remoteness of that husband—here Hallam as the figure in the absolutely masculine position, the position of the subject presumed to know—is perceived as kindness even though it looks like cruelty.

Like the withered violet, the symbolic embodiment of her playing and singing, the wife is a living memorial to a dead—and deadly—relationship. Yet it is precisely the witheredness of the violet, the symbol that has emptied into a fetish, that enables her fixed faith, her undying love, to arise. By cherishing the emptiness, playing and singing, she survives her husband's absence in life (his absence of mind, of care, of love) as Tennyson survives Hallam's absence in death. She survives, moreover, by maintaining the ideality of her husband's image despite the rejecting judgment of the "faithless people." More than he deserves, the husband is the product of his wife's vision as "she dwells on him with faithful eyes." Without her he would simply vanish into the mountain mists of his own narcissism, just as, without the imperfectly virile Tennyson, Hallam the virile master would simply vanish into the mists of eternity.

Tennyson, then, harbors the wish to be woman here not only in order to make good his failure at the absolutely masculine position, but also to repossess that position from another perspective, a perspective only seemingly inferior. He wishes for castration in order to receive the phallus. Or, more exactly, in order *to have received* the phallus, which, once received, need never be relinquished. The contrast between the wife's household knowledge and the husband's knowledge of a thousand things becomes deeply ironic in this light. If the beloved man sees only "his own vast shadow glory-crowned," what he does not see, what the crown of glory conceals, is that he sees only a blown-up reflection. The truth of his image escapes him; it is possessed instead by the woman who sees him see, and in so doing confirms him as a seer.

The domestic ideology of the poem may not become less distasteful through these ironies, but it surely becomes less inert. Tennyson may embrace gender polarity here, but he does not leave it as intact as Gauguin and Schreber do; there will be no short circuit, after all. Nor does Tennyson's anger—at Hallam for dying, at absolute masculinity for alienating the subject from nature, romance, and affection—get lost. On the contrary: the details of the husband's slights to his wife's heart combine to give the overt sentimentality of the poem some rough edges. Turned at a slight angle, this poem uses gender polarity to indict itself.

Riddles of the Sphinx

How best to formulate the paradox of Oedipal masculinity, the phallic instrument of sexual violence? I become a man by becoming an impostor—a male impersonator: I internalize the man I can never be and then play him to an audience of women. I stand to other men as a coconspirator, tacitly sharing my act with them as they share theirs with me. To women I stand as my superego stands to me. I become a subject by making women subject, through me, not so much to the name as to the voice of the Father: punitive, caressing, authoritative, indulgent, knowing, protective, terrible. Culturally, masculinity is my right to do this. Psychically, though, this right is no more than a rite, a coup de théâtre. Masculinity is a defense mechanism.

Straight and Narrow

Homophobia is an Oedipal institution, a means by which men can avoid the recognition that their masculinity is a defense mechanism. By conjoining the polarity of straight and gay with a polarity of perfect and defective masculinity, the straight man can find in his difference from the gay one the sign of his unbroken virility—precisely what he can never find in himself. The sign can then be passed reassuringly among a band of brothers across the medium of the outcast homosexual body that is now cast as effeminate. In this guise, homophobia also allows a certain departure from misogyny. Men can avoid hating (straight) women overmuch if they can hate gay men as much as they like.

Tuning up: The "Kreutzer" Sonata

The violinist Trukhachevski plays on the strings of Pozdnyshev's wife, which is to say on her nervous system, the exquisite excitability of which had been for a century or more the nexus of music and hysteria. In her own playing the wife redoubles on the piano strings this fiddling on her nerves, the fibers of her being, the web of sexuality in which her husband is ensnared. (Compare T. S. Eliot: "A woman drew her long black hair out tight / And fiddled whisper music on those strings.") Pozdnyshev is perfectly right to see the performance of the "Kreutzer" Sonata as an act of adultery. This sonata is a sexual appliance. Its performance is a sexual act that sexualizes—or rather resexualizes—all the apparently less dangerous music in its vicinity. In its sensory fullness, emotional violence, and intricate, passionate intertwining of instrumental voices, the "Kreutzer" Sonata breaks the bounds of genteel piano performance proper to women. Once that happens, nothing is safe. Nothing can keep the simple little piece played later, the little extra piece that forces the fatal outcome, from revealing itself to be what all music seeks to become, a thinly veiled erotic abyss.

Music is the speech of the female body, the female genitals; it must be fetishized, handed a prosthetic phallus, before men can tolerate it. Anything with a point will serve; Pozdnyshev finds that the handiest fetish is a knife. (Understandable, says the court: not guilty.) Later on his language, an oral performance replacing the manual one, replaces the knife. If only the wife had not been tempted to play this "Kreutzer" Sonata, or better yet, had not been able to play it! The nineteenth-century piano is given to Woman as a vehicle for the sublimation of her sexuality, which in turn is the vehicle by which her family is ritually unified. A good bourgeois wife is always also a musician—but a bad one.

The Soundtrack of the Sirens: Prague to Hollywood

Does that mean a good musician must be a bad wife? The myth of the sirens says so, but everybody knows how easy it is to defeat a siren: you just stuff your ears. (Pozdnyshev must have known that, too, yet he refused to let his wife cancel her performance. Foolish man, he wanted to hear that legendary song.) But nothing, of course, is quite that simple. Count on Franz Kafka, a man much bothered by sirens, to grasp the fact. In his parable "The Silence of the Sirens," Kafka explains that the sirens are most dangerous not when they sing, but when they don't. They did not, for example, sing for Ulysses; he just thought they did. Kafka's Ulysses, unlike Homer's Odysseus, stuffs his own ears with wax, not those of his crew; he triumphs in the false belief that he has been deaf to a song that was never sung. (Probably he knew, says Kafka, that the sirens' song could easily penetrate the wax; he was simply so charmed by his own cleverness that he forgot it.) The triumph of this Ulysses is merely a fantasy. The trouble is, merely this fantasy is a triumph. The sirens themselves are seduced by it; they want to "hold as long as they [can] the radiance that fell from Ulysses's great eyes." You can defeat a siren by being narcissistic. Just assume, on no ground whatever, that she must want to sing to you—you above all.

The ins and outs of Kafka's parable would make great musical comedy, and in one sense actually did so. Howard Hawks's movie *Gentlemen Prefer Blondes* is about a pair of sirens, played by Jane Russell and Marilyn Monroe, who sing their way to both love and money, which they can gain—this is 1953—only through marriage. Song is very much the medium of the women's desire and their seductiveness alike. Monroe's signature number is the once-famous "Diamonds Are a Girl's Best Friend"; Russell's is "Ain't Anyone Here for Love," a poolside extravaganza in which her character roves avidly through the scantily clad ranks of the men's Olympic swim team. This scene is an unwitting burlesque of the passage from "Song of Myself" in which the lonely young woman imagines herself frolicking in the sea with twenty-eight naked young men. (It's a man's fantasy of a woman's fantasy.) Monroe's character, however, the aptly named Lorelei Lee, is at her most sirenical in a scene where she does not sing. It is a farcical scene, not a sexy one—the seductress's equivalent to a figure skater's technical program. Trying to sneak out of an ocean liner's stateroom after stealing some sexually incriminating photographs, Lorelei gets stuck in a porthole. Like a mermaid or a siren (half woman, half bird), she is neatly bisected, divided into a good half, the upper body with its generous breasts and pouting, large-mouthed face, and a bad half, the lower body, still engaged in nefarious activity and figuratively localizing the unrepresentable and threatening "hole" of the female genitals.

In this posture Lorelei has two visitors, the ten-year-old "Mr. Spofford" (who has earlier remarked at dinner with Monroe and Russell that he is old enough to know a good-looking woman and does not plan to miss any meals) and the pudgy, doddering Piggy Beekman, an old diamond tycoon whom Lorelei is trying to snare. To disguise Lorelei's situation from Piggy, Mr. Spofford drapes a blanket from her neck and takes the place, behind it, of her lower body. He thus supplies Lorelei with a little man between her (absent) legs; he becomes the phallus. Piggy is a little suspicious of the substitution, but he wants to be fooled by it. Like Kafka's Ulysses, he charms himself with a stratagem— thus revealing his desires to be piggy indeed. Lorelei also turns out to be a Circe, another one of Ulysses' dangerous girlfriends.

Ulysses-Piggy tests the waters by asking to hold Lorelei's hand. What he gets is Mr. Spofford's, which turns out to be just as good; holding "her" hand, Piggy admires, Piggy desires, Lorelei. The sheer artifice of this masculine desire is obvious: what arouses it is not a woman but a simulacrum, a phantasm of femininity behind which the phallus is concealed. It is also obvious that this desire, if satisfied by its "true" object, would be pederastic. Indeed, this is too obvious: it undercuts the display of Monroe's (and Russell's) bodies and exposes the anxiety underlying a film that centers its big set piece on the display of near-naked male bodies but that regards desire between men as unrepresentable, indeed unthinkable. The transaction between a too-young and a too-old male, focused on an imaginary part of an imaginary body, suggests that femininity is an empty term throughout the male life cycle. Ulysses could see the sirens' "throats rising and falling, their breasts lifting, their eyes filled with tears" (431) as they sang even though none of this happened and there was no song. Piggy sees the seductress of his dreams even though her veil is in the wrong place.

But the wrong place is the right place. Masculine desire, the scene suggests, can be based entirely on fantasy provided that one real condition is met, the concealment of the woman's lower body. (The facial veil of the traditional seductress is a transposition of this condition to the upper body.) The concealment allows the phallus to lurk, which in turn allows desire to appear. Hence the Kafkaesque irony of the film's narrative: the women trade on the commodity value of their lower bodies in order to achieve the condition, marriage, of that value's loss. Marriage entails the renunciation of fantasy. True, the sirens refuse the modesty proper to brides and claim victory at the end by singing their way through a showy double wedding, but their razzmatazzz is just a swan song. They will soon be mere women; their story is over; they are no longer interesting. Desire needs another temptress, another movie. This conclusion, the 'fifties version of the taming of the shrew, is foreshadowed when Mr. Spofford, young Oedipus, pulls Lorelei out of the porthole and leaves her "all bruised." Russell is also yanked unceremoniously out of the water at the end of her siren scene. Male pleasure, a figurative coming, appears when a manhandled woman is abruptly expelled from the fantasy space of her seductiveness. The woman's "outing" reveals that she ultimately belongs to the social order that constrains her—and constrains her to desire it—by finally showing her being roughed up a little.

Ruling Bodies

Misogyny is always ugly. But there seems to be a consensus that modern misogyny, misogyny since the Enlightenment, is especially ugly, more vehement, more virulent than its antecedents. One reason why may be a historical change in the character of masculine empowerment. The Enlightenment inaugurates a turn from traditional patriarchy to what Juliet Flower McCannell calls the regime of the brother. This turn consists in the replacement of the paternal prince by the autonomous fraternal individual as the dominant figure of political and personal authority. Only after this replacement, in an era when the prince is ipso facto a tyrant, when tyranny has become a primary mode of transgression, and therefore of unspeakable pleasure, does the credo of the Marquis de Sade make sense: "Every man wants to be a tyrant when he fornicates." Modern misogyny understands desire as a form of tyranny, tyranny as the form of desire.

In traditional patriarchy, the prince is assumed to hold the position of absolute masculinity; he stands in the public place of the superego. The prince becomes the exception to the rule that no one can hold this position, and this exemption justifies the fact that other men, the subjects subject to the prince, can never hold it. The subject can thus be plausibly content with a finite power that is, as far as women go, more than ample. By vacating the prince's exemption, the modern era turns the subject's failure to hold the absolute position into something intolerable. There is suddenly no reason the position should not be held. Thus it becomes the object of masculine quest, the modern form of the holy grail, the King Solomon's mine of infinite empowerment and pleasure.

But infinite desire always stymies finite men—that much is a cliché. It was the nineteenth century that made it so, and instructively as far as gender goes. In Robert Browning's poem "Two in the Campagna," a man justifies jilting a woman (or a woman a man, it's tellingly hard to tell) by invoking the contrast between "infinite passion, and the pain / Of finite hearts that yearn." Apply this formula to power as well as love, or more exactly to the power relations that uphold love, and the modern situation clarifies itself. In Nietzsche's application, the sexual love of man for woman is an idealized form of "avarice," an anxiety-laden lust for possession. The equation draws at least some of its power from the impression that Nietzsche, rarely or never a lover, is trying to posture as he has been told a lover should: "The lover desires unconditional and sole possession of the person for whom he longs; he desires equally unconditional power over the soul and over the body of the beloved; he alone wants to be loved and desires to live and rule in the other soul as supreme and supremely desirable" (88–89). In fantasy, the lover is a supreme ruler and the supreme ruler is a tyrant; he, the lover-tyrant, is his own "dragon guarding [the] golden hoard as the most inconsiderate and selfish of all 'conquerers' and exploiters" (89). In fantasy only, however: for possession, says Nietzsche, inevitably wearies the possessor and spurs him on to desire new possession, fuller possession. No woman can surrender herself unconditionally enough to satisfy any man; even a man who can force her to do anything cannot force her to do that. The basis of modern misogyny is the unbearable finitude of masculine power.

Bad Signs

Rape is commonplace; castration is news. Why, to take a contemporary instance, should Lorena Bobbitt's cutting off her husband's penis have caused a titter of national proportions and instantly become an American folk legend? Why did being the victim make the improbably but aptly named John Wayne Bobbitt a celebrity? No woman has ever become a celebrity for being raped. Bobbitt's suffering, of course, is not in question here; his curious privilege is.

Perhaps sexual violence is noteworthy only when it disturbs our habitual ways of representing the world we live in. By that standard, sexual violence against women would tend to be normalized, anesthetized, even among those who genuinely deplore it; the abused female body is a normal, even prototypical, object of representation. In the nineteenth century you can find high-cultural spokesmen who will not mince words about this. Not even Whitman is immune from the gendered crossing of representation with sadistic pleasure, and Émile Zola is positively urbane about it:

> By the city dead-house by the gate,
> As idly sauntering wending my way from the clangor,
> I curious pause, for lo, an outcast form, a poor dead
>   prostitute brought,
> Her corpse they deposit unclaim'd, it lies on the damp brick
>   pavement,
> The divine woman, her body, I see the body, I look on it
>   alone . . .
> Fair, fearful wreck—tenement of a soul—itself a soul,
> Unclaim'd, avoided house—take one breath from my
>   tremulous lips,
> Take one tear dropt aside as I go for thought of you,
> Dead house of love—house of madness and sin, crumbled,
>   crush'd,
> House of life, erewhile talking and laughing—but ah, poor
>   house, dead even then,
> Months, years, an echoing, garnish'd house—but dead, dead,
>   dead.
>
> *Whitman, "The City Dead House"*

Sometimes gangs of small boys came in [to the Paris Morgue], who rushed along the [display] windows and only stopped in front of female corpses. They leaned on the glass with their hands and ran their impudent eyes over the bare breasts, nudging each other and passing smutty remarks, learning vice at the school of death. Young louts have their first women in the Morgue.

Zola, Thérèse Raquin 111

Despite his assertions, and despite his unquestionably real sympathy, Whitman does not see the prostitute's body at all. What he sees, and seizes—claims, as in claiming the body—is an opportunity to prolong a metaphor, a strangely moralistic metaphor coming from him. In so doing, he also prolongs both the casual curiosity to which he (the idler, the saunterer) confesses and the acute bodily sensations—the quickened breathing, tremulousness, welling of tears—from whose erotically tinted pleasure he averts his gaze. Zola also moralizes, but the narrative movement of his paragraph, from hands on glass to eyes on breasts to nudging and smutty remarks, reenacts for the reader the sexual adventure it describes. Like it or not, Zola is just one of the boys. The glass at the Morgue that frames the women's bodies as public spectacles becomes the enabling surface of representation through which sexual pleasure passes. Hence the unapologetic closing metaphor: the eye, no less than the penis, can be the instrument of male sexual initiation, so long as its object is safely under glass.

Sexual violence against women, then, would become news only when it somehow disrupts the order of representation, the order in which subjectivity is framed and regulated. If a popular actress is pursued by a stalker, the broadcasting of the stalker's desire will also reveal the aggressiveness latent in the desire of the "normal" men who are fans of the actress, perhaps fantasists about her, but who would never pursue her themselves. Worse yet, the identity of the stalker as a fan himself reveals that the whole apparatus of celebrity representation plays dangerously with the aggressive-possessive substrate of all desire. Similarly, the tabloid obsession with the "murder" of Marilyn Monroe converts her death into a sex crime, the dark outcome of her famous combination of seductiveness and vulnerability.

Such are the exceptions. Sexual violence against men, however, disturbs representation whenever it happens, with no exceptions. It is, in effect, violence against representation itself. (Historically, this statement refers only to white men. No "negro" or other Other ever became a celebrity by being lynched; subjugated non-white bodies are another normal object of representation.) A Bobbitt-inspired cartoon in *The New Yorker* captures this point very well. The three blind mice, white mice wearing dark glasses and propping themselves on canes, sit on chairs around a radio. With a stricken look, one exclaims: "She cut off his *what* with a carving knife?" The real joke here is precisely about blindness, the blindman's bluff of representation. What the mouse sees, and sees he can no longer play at not seeing, is that the story of the three blind mice, his story, has been about castration, his castration, all along. Hence the radio: for this is news, representation's cover is blown, its overvaluation of the phallus flashes before the blindest of eyes.

In My Second

wolf dream the maternal figure of the older woman is locked away from the scene of desire, an anti-Oedipal scene placed outside the home. The lurking masculine figure, the figure of the father's desire, of my own Oedipal desire, is invasive in this scene, a trespasser in a venue not his own. He violently seeks to appropriate the young woman, the nonmaternal beloved of my scene of desire, but in return I displace him—literally dis-place him, send him back home—both satirically in the image of the "dandling" bears, turning the name of the father to Baby Bear, or Teddy Bear, and lyrically in the image of the wolf in which the brutal motion of rape is replaced by a lightfooted frolic in the snow.

Heterosexless Desire

"What was terrible, you know"—thus Pozdnyshev—"was that I considered myself to have a complete right to [my wife's] body as if it were my own, and yet at the same time I felt I could not control that body, that it was not mine and she could dispose of it as she pleased, and that she wanted to dispose of it not as I wished her to" (418). It would be hard to find a better or clearer statement of the gender-polarized masculine desire to control feminine sexuality. This desire is often said to stem from fear of a feminine *jouissance* that threatens, Medusa-like, to petrify the man who confronts it. But although such fear can no doubt enhance the desire for control, or serve to rationalize it, Pozdnyshev's statement points to a deeper, more impersonal cause.

Gender-polarized men like Pozdnyshev seek to control feminine sexuality, not because they are afraid of it, but because they are afraid of life without it, which is exactly the life they are constrained to lead. The femininity constituted by gender polarity cannot be eroticized; it can never satisfy the desire it arouses. As

Pozdnyshev's statement suggests, polarized masculine desire can either be narcissistic, directed toward the woman as an extension of the man's own body or body-ego, or rivalrous, directed towards the woman as the potential object of someone else's desire. What it cannot be is erotic, directed towards the woman as the subject of her own desire. Insofar as women claim erotic interests in this sense, they either cease to be desirable (Pozdnyshev observes that his wife "is not in her first youth, has lost a side-tooth, and [has] a slight puffiness about her [416]), or they assume a desirability that is monstrous. In the logic of polarity, the masculine can desire the feminine physically, but not erotically.

Granted: at first glance this formula seems bizarre. Everyone knows that male gender dominance goes hand in hand with male erotic dominance. But what does this truism mean?

It means that the social order is geared to serve male genital interests in women. Which is surely so. But sexuality, even for those unfriendly to psychoanalysis, cannot plausibly be identified with genitality. Sexuality covers the whole field of interest in which fantasy and desire intertwine. It comes about in psychical life—and this, I would say with Jean Laplanche, is Freud's great discovery about it—precisely when desire detaches itself from bodily need. Erotic sexuality conducts the desire thus liberated into the sphere of the subject's recognition by itself and others. The stake in erotic sexuality is not someone else's body but someone else's desire, the exchange of desire for desire. (Hence nineteenth-century representations of sexuality as a precious liquid or semiliquid material, which Freud would call libido and Whitman the "body electric.")

But the exchange of desire for desire can pass only between two subjects, not between a desiring masculine subject and de-

sired feminine object. Accordingly, in the regime of gender polarity, erotic sexuality can appear under only two conditions: it
must either temporarily suspend polarity or be homosexual.
Otherwise, insofar as a man objectifies a woman whether by
glamorizing or debasing her; insofar as he fixes on her body as the
repository of a threatening-alluring otherness; insofar as he acts
with tacit reference to the desire of a virile rival, the character
of his desire is not sexual but social, not libidinal and fluid but
egoistic and structural. What such desire seeks is possession of
the phallus; sexuality is only a means to that end, or rather, since
the end can never be realized, a means of fantasizing, imagining,
representing it. Representation, indeed, often usurps even the
physical pressure of sexuality in this venue. This is the realm
of woman's body as the object of modeling, body sculpture, inscription, taking in everything from genital mutilation in non-
Western cultures to the history of corseting—now called diet-
ing—in the West.

But a caution is in order here. Despite its inclination to abuse,
this phallic regime has a powerful imaginary appeal to both men
and women. ("I cannot remember a time," writes Daphne Merkin, "when I didn't . . . fantasize about being reduced to a craven
object of desire by a firm male hand" [99]. The fantasy of abjection in a "self-aware . . . putatively independent-minded woman"
[99] has general resonance; Merkin's particular, preferred form
of abjection, a fine emblem of gender polarity, is being spanked.)
The regime, moreover, is just as effective with the repressed as
with the "emancipated," with the prudish as with the libertine.
Its alternatives are still too fugitive, too marginal, and too poorly
described to produce a viable ideal. It is not likely to disappear
any time soon. Yet even so: it can still be deauthorized, still be

dislodged as a normative and often unconscious principle of social organization, still be rendered vulnerable to displacement
and modification, even appropriation, by gender synergy. As a
social ideal, gender synergy seeks to overturn the rule of gender
polarity; as a social practice, gender synergy allows us—among
other things—to play at gender polarity.

"*I Wanna Be a Football Hero*"

In the aftermath of O. J. Simpson's alleged murder, Pozdnyshev style, of his allegedly battered wife, Nicole Brown Simpson, and her companion Ronald Goldman, an expert commentator on public television made a bemused observation. Men who batter women, she said, are often competent, responsible, congenial people in every other department of their lives. (Just like Pozdnyshev.) They are abnormal only in their proclivity to sexual violence. (Just like Pozdnyshev.)

Such exceptionalism, if true, would be bemusing indeed. Why would so many men have only a single abnormal patch, and why always this one same patch? The real truth about these men is that they are normal in *every* department of their lives: their sexual violence is normal, too. Or, to be more exact, the imaginary masculinity that rationalizes their violence is built into the structure of normality, where it comes into conflict with social and moral codes that prohibit acts of violence. One reason why sexually violent men feel justified during their acts is that defying the prohibition feels heroic. Remember Pozdnyshev and his scimitar, the prosthesis that transforms the shoeless killer into a grand Turk or Tartar, despite his losing its scabbard behind a bourgeois sofa. Remember the tinny ring of Whitman's second-hand boast, "I do not hurt you any more than is necessary."

Aubade

I can never recall my "Rosamunde" dream without also recalling some lines from Robert Browning's poem "By the Fireside":

> By the rose-flesh mushrooms, undivulged
>> Last evening—nay, in today's first dew
> Yon sudden coral nipple bulged.
>
>> *ll. 61–63*

The quotation dwells on, lingers over, the sudden bulging of the coral nipple, an image that screens a memory with the lightest of veils. The woodland in the dream resembled a park where I had recently had a romantic picnic. The poetic image condenses the visible effects of desire on both my body (a man's) and my partner's (a woman's). A kind of bulge in memory, the poetic image recaptures the erotic fervor underlying the dream image of yellow-pink roses: a fervor of pure reciprocity in which each body is marked by the same tangible and visible sign, in which the lower body of one partner rhymes with the upper body of the other, in which sexual dualism collapses into an arresting singularity, in which "heterosexual" partners share a "homosexual" pleasure.

The color of the sign adds its own resonance: the coral in the poem, the yellow-pink of roses in the dream, both approximate the pale rose color of the blouse my partner wore. And from color a filament runs through word and image to music: the coral of the poetic image alludes to both the color and the flower of the dream, which reappear with heightened sensuousness and lyricism in the tune from Schubert's *Rosamunde*.

This fusion of lyricism and sensuousness is deeply pleasurable; it wants to be idealized, perhaps deservedly so. And yet look how this dream reproduces the scene but not the partner of a pleasure shared. Look how—at least on one reading—it phallicizes the pleasure itself, not just in visualizing an erectile shape, but in privileging the effects of an "arresting singularity." The dream wants to recapture a moment of mutual, uncoerced happiness, but wants, just as much, to take sole possession of that moment: to control its significance, to retrieve it from its feminine sharer by making her only a secret sharer, a diffuse, disembodied presence, music on a soundtrack.

The dream as cultural text: this one perhaps reveals what lyricism is in general, the latent activity of a disavowed feminine partner. But perhaps, too, the sense of longing in the dream regrets that disavowal, is a longing for a recovery of avowal, a lyricism the richer for being deconstructed. I don't know. I'd like to think so.

Ah! But

in both of my wolf dreams I have no fixed position, no single embodiment: multiple, dispersed, I scintillate like the snow in moonlight, the sun at the back of the narrator-wolf: I am *jouissance*.

Cyanosis

When Pozdnyshev feels repelled by the unattractiveness of his wife on her deathbed, what else is he feeling? Surprise, for one thing: dead and dying women were notoriously seductive for nineteenth-century men. The bodies of such women, imaginary ones anyway, were felt to combine the pliancy of flesh with the perfection of sculpture, making the death of women at once a form of art and a form of sex. (Judging by tabloid photography of Nicole Brown Simpson, not much has changed.) Similarly, one contemporary reports that dead women's faces "[took] on an expression of pain made so noble and almost so sympathetic by their suffering that it allowed an otherworldly happiness to shine through which could often only be compared to the miraculous expression of a woman who is in love to the point of ecstasy" (Dijkstra 54). *To* the point but not *at* the point: death spiritualizes the woman by infinitely deferring the effect of her orgasm, at once offering her sexuality to the man's gaze and denying it to her enjoyment. (He consumes her *jouissance* by monumentalizing it in the symbolic order.) Zola's brutal remark about the sexual initiation in the Paris morgue says the same thing more honestly.

The source of this necro-voyeurism is less the desire for complete feminine passivity than it is the wish to be absolved of responsibility toward women as human beings. "It is not I," says the necro-voyeur, "who petrifies this woman into a mere object of visual pleasure; it is Death."

With Pozdnyshev the formula is reversed. "I, Death," he says, "enflesh this object of visual pleasure into a mere woman." Pozdnyshev at one level kills his wife in order to be repelled rather than aroused by her. Repulsion secures the masculine position that desire has always subverted. Repelled, Pozdnyshev can be feminized by neither the desire he feels in himself nor the desire he projects into other men and feels as jealousy. What he sees at the deathbed is thus "first and most of all" the disfiguration that marks his imperviousness to desire. In an earlier spate of rage, he has hurled a paperweight at his wife and dashed an inkwell to the floor; now it is as if her face were a paper blotched by ink, a parody of a legal document attesting to his mastery: "What struck me first and most of all was her bruised and swollen face, blue on part of the nose and under the eyes" (427–28).

Only by her coffin, three days later, does Pozdnyshev feel remorse at the sight of his wife's face, now no longer described as marked by his hand. Where the bruise on a dying face was the sign of his mastery, the lividity on a dead one is the sign of his guilt; repetrified, it petrifies. Yet even here the effect is not debasing but exalting: Pozdnyshev undergoes a "spiritual conversion" and becomes the archetypal masculine figure we have seen him to be, the Wandering Jew–Flying Dutchman–Ancient Mariner with hypnotically glittering eyes who goes about the world seeking forgiveness by telling his story, and who, failing to find what he seeks—because no amount of forgiveness could ever satisfy him—greedily sucks in perpetual clouds of cigarette smoke as a substitute.

Homoerogenous Zones

Modern homophobia shares in the positional logic of modern misogyny and therefore in its violence. Because the affectionate element in male social bonding can always slide over into sexuality (in Eve Sedgwick's terms, because homosocial relations cannot reliably be divided from homosexual ones), the masculine subject defined by gender polarity is haunted by the possibility that even the most manly things about him may be tacitly marked by effeminacy. The need to disavow this possibility gives a general legitimacy to the more or less violent debasement of gay men. The legitimacy is so powerful that it does not even need to be rationalized; being a homophobe means never having to say you're sorry. (Being a misogynist means that "sorry" is supposed to get you off the hook.)

Twentieth-century gender polarity has been so severe that any sexually ambiguous behavior by men may immediately be stigmatized as a sign of possible homosexuality. The nineteenth century allowed for other possibilities. Writers like Tennyson

and Whitman tried to open up a "middle zone" of masculine affection, in which behavior normally sanctioned only between
men and women was allowable as long as it clearly stopped
short—how short was highly variable—of genital (which is to say
genital-oral or genital-anal) consummation.

Tennyson's representations of Arthur Hallam's speech as a
sweet, refreshing liquid create a tightly circumscribed pleasure-
space in which in which the privileged listener can drink in the
rich liquescence, or bask in it. Close bodily proximity, suffused
by expressive utterance, becomes a form of loving touch. One
result is to invest literal touch, however technically innocent,
with an extra charge of intimacy and pleasure. *In Memoriam* is
haunted by the loss not only of Hallam's voice but also of his
handclasp. Most of the poems in the sequence arise to fill the gap
between the loss of that handclasp and its imaginary recovery:

> Doors, where my heart was used to beat
> So quickly, waiting for a hand,
>
> A hand that can be clasped no more—
> Behold me . . .
>
> 7, ll. 3–6

> Doors, where my heart was used to beat
> So quickly, not as one that weeps
> I come once more. . . .
>
> And in my thought with scarce a sigh
> I take the pressure of [his] hand.
> *119*, ll. 1–3, 11–12

Real or imagined, a touch can at times open subliminal vistas of
an even closer contact:

> Descend, and touch, and enter; hear
> The wish too strong for words to name.
>
> *93*, ll. 13–14

The unspeakable wish in these lines is not for a spiritual union best symbolized by erotic imagery; it is for an erotic union miraculously transposed into the register of spirit.

Whitman, too, builds the middle zone of homoerogenous affection around fantasies of oral and tactile pleasure, but the pleasures he builds on are more corporeal than their counterparts in Tennyson. Manly love seeks to express itself publicly by kissing, handholding, and embracing:

> [Now] comes one a Manhattanese and ever at parting kisses
>   me lightly on the lips with robust love,
> And I on the crossing of the street or on the ship's deck give a
>   kiss in return,
> We observe that salute of American comrades land and sea,
> We are those two natural and nonchalant persons.
>
> *"Behold This Swarthy Face" ll. 4–7*

> A leaf for hand in hand;
> You natural persons old and young!. . . .
> You friendly boatmen and mechanics! you roughs!. . . .
> I wish to infuse myself among you till I see it common for
>   you to walk hand in hand.
>
> *"A Leaf for Hand in Hand" ll. 1–2, 4, 6*

Seemingly more candid than Tennyson's, the loving gestures imagined by Whitman are in one sense more restrictive. Their erotic literalness requires an especially strict enforcement of the genital proviso. Although Whitman does acknowledge wishes too strong for words to name, and in one poem even enjoins the "confession drops," the "blushing drops," of his desires to "stain [his] every page" ("Trickle Drops" ll. 6, 11), his subliminal vistas are few and far between. In recompense, however, his small vignettes of manly love allow the affectionate element in male social bonding to slide over into sexuality without a murmur—except of pleasure.

The genital proviso was tacit, but enabling; love could flourish in all regions but one. And because the middle zone greatly expanded the range of available masculine positions, it greatly diminished the need for misogyny. The fluid positionality created by the possibility of unpunished affection between men removed the necessity—though not the persistent tendency—to punish the same kind of fluidity between men and women.

"It glides quickly in through my ears"

What must Tolstoy be hearing in the Presto of Beethoven's "Kreutzer" Sonata? Passion and impetuosity on the surface, and lots of them; then the visceral effect of instrumental writing that summons up and magnifies the raw physicality of making music, above all in an urgent mutual rhythm that punctuates the score with accentual thrusts, the full weight of the players' bodies repeatedly borne down on the bodies of their instruments in unison or alternation; then a degree of intimate, deeply attentive interplay that exceeds anything a Pozdnyshev, or perhaps a Tolstoy, could ever share with his wife. It does not matter that this Presto sounds nothing at all like conventional "love music"; there is a palpable erotic script in its duo writing.

In Beethoven's day, with the performers presumptively male, it is a homoerotic script, something like a celebration of passionate friendship that at its height becomes indistinguishable from passion itself. The Presto searches for the outer boundaries of homosocial partnership and leaves the players or listeners to say whether those boundaries have been crossed. By Tolstoy's day, with the piano anchoring the bourgeois drawing room, the erotic script is that of heterosexual seduction. The family piano, installed as a site where women give pleasure by acting out the constraints on their sexuality, constantly threatens to become the site where women take so much pleasure that their sexuality erupts. (The danger is especially great between teacher and student, professional and amateur; see Leppert for the full story.) Pozdnyshev even sees the piano as a sexual appliance, which Trukhachevski does little more than, so to speak, turn on:

> The door to the dancing room is shut but I hear the sound of a rhythmic arpeggio and his and her voices. . . . I quickly opened the door. He was sitting at the piano playing those arpeggios with his large white upturned fingers. She was standing in the curve of the piano, bending over some open music. . . . She did not start or move but only blushed. (405)

It is as if the bending body of the woman harmonized with, blended itself into, the curve of the piano and the rhythm of the arpeggios. The sexual machine is the female body itself.

Latent Remedies

Sexual violence cannot be cured by making men aware of how brutal it is. They know how brutal it is. They also know that in *their* case the brutality was justified, that they were entitled to it even though they know it was wrong and now feel sorry about it. This alibi has proven both persistent and unbreakable. It has done so because the combination of entitlement and guilt is less the effect of sexual violence than its cause. The violator cycles between an imaginary identification with the superego, which offers the sense of entitlement, and symbolic subordination to the superego, which imposes the sense of guilt. Guilt, no matter how sincere, cannot break this cycle. Because the position in which we receive guilt is figured as feminine, the subject must retreat to entitlement in order to be (re)positioned as masculine. The cycle can be broken only by breaking the gendering of its positions. Guilt must be reconstructed as something other than symbolic castration, and masculinity reconstructed as something other than an identification with the symbolically uncastratable.

Similarly: men do not commit sexual violence because they are taught to cherish their aggressiveness, although they are, nor because their sexuality involves them in the objectification of women, although it does. (Any straight man who says he never objectifies women is a liar. But then again, any gay man who says he never objectifies men is a liar. Sexuality makes liars of us all.) Nor, *pace* Catharine MacKinnon, do men commit sexual violence because pornographic imagery sends "direct messages" to their penises (21). (True, the idea of a thinking penis is intriguing, but it is doubtless not what MacKinnon has in mind.) No: sexual violence is a product of moral passion. It will stop only if we can learn how to change the psychodynamics of morality. That change cannot come from a simple reversal: sensitivity for aggressiveness, personalization for objectification. The mandate of reversal would be unenforceable in any case; the opposites would keep on evoking each other dialectically. The change must come instead from the enhanced experience of gender synergy, the opening of all subject-positions to all genderings, the recasting of all terms of gender as provisional and mutable. Under the regime of gender polarity, in which we live whether we like it or not, such synergy occurs where discourse or imagery or social practice say more than they know, or seek to say more than they know how to: as when Walt Whitman, not quite knowing (how), shows in one poem—we've seen it already—that he wants to suck at his father's breast and, in another, that he wants to submit himself blissfully to his mother's law:

> The old face of the mother of many children,
> Whist! I am fully content. . . .

She sits in the armchair under the shaded porch of the
   farmhouse,
The sun just shines on her old white head.

Her ample gown is of cream-hued linen,
Her grandsons raised the flax, and her grand-daughters spun
   it with the distaff and the wheel.

The melodious character of the earth,
The finish beyond which philosophy cannot go and does not
   wish to go,
The justified mother of men.

"Faces" ll. 68–69, 78–84

The Law Is an Ass

There are moments when the truth about gender polarity flashes out with startling clarity. In 1724 an Englishman named William Yonge petitioned the Houses of Parliament for a divorce from his wife, Mary, on grounds of adultery. But the man who cast himself before Parliament as a poor cuckold was known to the rest of London as an infamous libertine. What Yonge was really after was the pleasure of parading his wife's sexuality in public—and of taking her money. (He got both.) The case moved Lady Mary Wortley Montagu to write a poem imagining Mary's Yonge's reply, the high point of which is a stinging accusation:

> Beneath the shelter of the law you stand,
>   And urge my ruin with a cruel hand,
> While to my fault thus rigidly severe,
> Tamely submissive to the man you fear.
>   *"Epistle from Mrs. Yonge to Her Husband"*
>   *ll.* 55−59

Montagu does not quite say, or know how to say, that Yonge's tame submission is what feeds his cruelty to his wife, or that his cruelty is the instrument he uses to blind himself to his servility. But she knows what she sees, and she sees what she cannot say.

Ménages à Trois

Jealousy is Pozdnyshev's first line of defense against desire. Tru-khachevski at first is a perfect conduit for jealousy, an unparal-leled stroke of good luck. He is a musician and therefore some-one who performs sex in public, caressing his instrument and making exposed bosoms heave; he is a disreputable ne'er-do-well, not above charming other men's wives; and he is a figure of slightly excessive fleshiness who inspires Pozdnyshev with the homoerotic fascination, noted earlier, that latches onto the vio-linist's red lips and bulging bottom.

Were Trukhachevski to seduce Pozdnyshev's wife, the abused husband could rid himself of both heterosexual desire, by dis-placing it into jealousy, and homosexual desire, by displacing it into the other man's heterosexual desire. The displacement, a kind of visceral expulsion, would be further facilitated by the im-agery of racial abjection through which Pozdnyshev distances himself from both his wife and his rival: the one a typical woman, battening on masculine desire the way Jews batten on money-

lending (373), the other a Hottentot queen. So the husband sets
about arranging the seduction of his wife, not by design but by
compulsion:

> [Trukhachevski could] twist [my wife] round his little finger
> and do what he liked with her. I could not help seeing this
> and I suffered terribly. But for all that, or perhaps on account
> of it, some force obliged me against my will to be not merely
> polite but amiable to him. . . . I gave him expensive wines at
> supper, went into raptures over his playing, spoke to him
> with a particularly amiable smile, and invited him to dine
> and play with my wife again the next Sunday. (404)

To become a cuckold may well be Pozdnyshev's strongest sexual
desire. It is striking in this connection that his first spate of murderous rage against his wife—the paperweight-inkwell episode—
erupts when she comes to his room offering to cancel her planned
performance with Trukhachevski because the plan upsets her
husband. He needs his jealousy so badly that if his wife takes it
away from him he'll kill her.

The trouble is that jealousy is not enough to purge desire.
(Shakespeare's Othello and Verdi's Otello also discover this.)
Pozdnyshev's jealousy displaces his desire but also preserves it,
returns it to him in reverse form. He needs so badly to get rid of
his jealousy that if his wife doesn't take it away from him he'll
kill her.

Ralph and Alice

In *The Princess*, Tennyson frames a lengthy debate over the boundaries of gender with the cross-dressing of a statue at the beginning and the undressing of the statue at the end. The scene is a picturesque ruin during a summer festival:

> there was Ralph himself,
> A broken statue propt against the wall,
> As gay as any. Lilia, wild with sport,
> Half child, half woman as she was, had wound
> A scarf of orange round his stony helm,
> And robed the shoulders in a rosy silk,
> That made the old warrior from his ivied nook
> Glow like a sunbeam.
>
> *Prologue ll. 98–105*

The narrator of this passage clearly enjoys the feminization of the old warrior, but his pleasure is more ambivalent than it seems at first—certainly more than its obvious component of Oedipal gloating would permit. The rhythm and sonority of the verse suggest a sensuous participation in the bright colors and smooth textures that enwrap the statue, but the general tone is sophisticated and lightly ironic. The contrast between the fetching drapery and the "stony helm" shows that the pleasure of Sir Ralph's feminization (which Ralph himself seems to share, "gay as any") is insubstantial; it is no match for the weight of virile authority that plays even about a broken statue in need of propping.

Inevitably, the end of the poem resolves the ambiguity as it resolves the debate. The latter resolution purges the worst crudities of Victorian misogyny without altering the underlying Oedipal dynamics that make them possible; as noted earlier, *The Princess* is no *In Memoriam*. The former resolution gives Ralph back his missing dignity, and, again inevitably, does so at the feminine hand that removed it:

> Last little Lilia, rising quietly,
> Disrobed the glimmering statue of Sir Ralph
> From those rich silks, and home well-pleased we went.
> *Canto 7, ll. 116–18*

The poem, a lesser *Don Giovanni*, ends with the triumph of the Father's law set in stone.

The logic of this reversal turns on the insufficiency of the crossed-dressed statue. Only thinly disguised here, this is a preponderantly genital logic, the bizarre but normative pattern of which has become familiar in feminist theory. Because men equate the penis with the phallus, they cannot see women as having a genital organ but only as lacking one, and therefore they see women as embodiments of lack in general. (We have explored their investment in feminine lack already.) Men, it follows, cannot see that women in reality lack nothing. In fact, they *must* not see this: ironically, masculine subjectivity depends on the constitutive presence of nothing other than a masculine lack, a failure of perception that, being a symbolic blindness, may also be a castration substitute.

In the symbolic order of modernity, for men to recognize women as without lack would be intolerable. For if women, lacking the imaginary phallus, nonetheless lack nothing, then women stand outside the entire order of masculine-feminine binaries. Women without lack, in other words, are immune from the dreaded condition to which men remain exquisitely vulnerable: femininity. When Lilia dresses up the statue, she is neither genderless nor gendered, neither child nor woman, but a "wild" subject full of her own wildness. In order to retain the Lilias of the world as bearers of the feminine, and at the same time to maintain themselves as heirs to the fiction of phallic masculinity, men must make it their business to manufacture feminine lack. They must imagine it, not only in women, but also in themselves, whenever they come to occupy a feminine position, no matter how gratifying. To enjoy old Sir Ralph in drag without the protection of irony is to identify too closely with his feminization; it lacks firmness. Men must even recruit women as their allies by encouraging them to identify with glamorized feminine positions. It must be "little Lilia" who disrobes the statue. Even those of us, men and women alike, who know that gender polarity is a coercive fiction, may be complicit in this project: much as we would like to, we cannot turn polarity to synergy just by flinging a scarf over it.

Ear to the Ground

What Tolstoy hears in the Presto of the "Kreutzer" Sonata is the dirty little secret of gender polarity—or it would be if the secret were not so open, like a gap or an edge in a piece of clothing that we agree not to notice as we keep surreptitiously gazing over or through it. ("How can that first Presto be played in a drawing-room among ladies in low-necked dresses?") What Tolstoy hears is the unspoken truth that gender polarity is a travesty, is travesty itself: that both of its opposing positions are feminine. When the music carries him away, takes him beyond himself, he is enabled to yield to this truth without speaking it, to enjoy it (in the sense of *jouissance*) without knowing it. That's why listening makes him so extraordinarily happy and why, on later reflection, it disgusts him so much: exactly the same process that he goes through with sex. "Music," says Pozdnyshev (we have heard it before) "carries me immediately and directly into the mental condition [of the man] who composed it. My soul merges with his and together with him I pass from one condition to another" (411). In the immediacy of listening, music is blissful submission, erotic merging with a superior man; afterwards, on reflection, it is debasement. Pozdnyshev describes this debasement as a forgetting of his "true position," and so it is, but not in the sense he means. The forgetting coincides with, and covers up, the acting-out of the truth of his true position. The truth is that the masculine position differs from the feminine only in being hysterical about its own femininity.

Tolstoy, hearing through Pozdnyshev, thus incidentally discovers one of the main purposes that listening to music—"just listening"—serves in the modern symbolic order. The listener in this order wants to obey the music, even to be loved by the music for obeying it, but does not want to want this. Listening works, accordingly, like a classic process of hysterical conversion; it resolves the listener's ambivalence by turning something voluntary, a desire to obey, into something involuntary, a commotion of feeling and sensation that the music is felt to impose. The listener cannot be responsible for what cannot be helped. Attitudes about music tend to vary according to whether the gender-polarized listener uses extra devices—aesthetic distance, concentration on form, relegation of music to the background of other activities—to stiffen the posture of listening. In the absence or failure of such props, listening is the abandonment of masculine pretension, a feminine abandon. In retrospect, when the impact of listening has faded, those who need to disavow this truth about it can do so by belittling the music.

Tinnitus

What Tolstoy does *not* hear in the Presto of the "Kreutzer" is something even more discomfiting than the presence of femininity on both sides of the gender bar. Pozdnyshev, Tolstoy's earpiece and the buzzing in his ear, a minotaur caught by his cuckold's horns at the vestibulum of the labyrinth, provides the desired deafness. What Tolstoy does not hear and could not bear to hear is the music's—is music's—gender synergy.

It speaks, that synergy, or sings, rather, in one particular passage, itself doubled as a requisite of form. This is the movement's lyrical second theme. Earlier, seeking to hear the gender-polarized masculinity of this movement, I treated this theme as a mere parenthesis. Now it is time to listen again, recognizing that a parenthesis, too, can make a difference—even a gender difference. A parenthesis can expand, even if only as a nimbus, to envelop the whole that contains it.

The contrast between the Presto's first and second themes conforms closely to the classic format for movements of its sonata-allegro type as described, or prescribed, by the nine-teenth-century German musicologist A. B. Marx:

> The first theme is the one determined at the outset, that is, with a primary freshness and energy—consequently that which is energetically, emphatically, absolutely shaped . . . the dominating and determining feature. On the other hand, the second theme . . . is the [idea] created afterward, serving as a contrast, dependent on and determined by the former—con-sequently, and according to its nature necessarily, the milder [idea], one more supple than emphatically shaped, as if it were feminine to that preceding masculine. In just this [gen-dered] sense each of the two themes is different, and only with one another [do they constitute something] higher, more perfect. (*Die Lehre* 221)

Marx's emphasis is not on masculine dominance, but on the complementarity of the genders, musical and otherwise, each of which is imperfect until the two join to form a balanced whole. But complementarity of this sort has historically served as a de-ceptive, often self-deceptive, ideal, the good face put on a hier-archical order. The point has been theorized for music by Susan McClary, who in effect identifies the feminine in music as ex-pressive dissonance, as that which demands resolution. In sonata forms like this one, the complementary themes are harmonically unequal. The first sounds in the music's primary key; the second is introduced in a secondary key and later resolved to the primary one, its feminine waywardness ultimately subdued to masculine order.

In the "Kreutzer" Presto, the second theme observes this po-larity in relation to the movement as a whole, but fosters a coun-

tervailing synergy among its own parts. "Feminine" in relation
to the first theme, the second theme is itself subdivided into masculine and feminine segments (see example 1a). The masculine,
which sounds first, is in the major and presents a chorale texture
in the piano with the "voices" in tenor-bass registers. The feminine follows in the minor with the voices of its parallel chorale
texture in the alto-soprano registers. The masculine segment is
longer, the feminine more expressive.

This internal gendering of the second theme both puts into
question the gender polarity of the movement as a whole—the
"feminine" term of which turns out to be two-thirds masculine
in itself—and also creates a musical image of true, nonhierarchical gender complementarity. This is best heard at the moment of
overall resolution, when the second theme returns in the primary
key (see example 1b). At this point the gendered voicing of the
piano's chorales are enhanced, the first segment's voices sounding deeper than before, the second segment's higher. The result
is a resonant space of gender synergy in which the formative processes of the entire movement momentarily crystallize.

This synergy ripples throughout the entire movement, as I
can show if I am indulged a few more technical details. On its
original appearance, the "feminine" segment of the second
theme appears in the minor mode of the secondary major key
(the dominant), which is introduced by the "masculine" segment.
Structurally, the feminine segment thus forms the most unstable
element in the movement's thematic makeup. The instability is
mirrored in the segment's own half-tranquil, half-rueful expressivity. On its recapitulation, however, the feminine segment
sounds in the minor mode of the major primary key (the tonic),
which is reintroduced by the masculine segment. As it happens,

Example 1. Beethoven, "Kreutzer" Sonata, first movement.
A. Second theme in exposition. B. Second theme in recapitulation.

B.

the movement as a whole is "in" the tonic minor, not the tonic major; structurally, the feminine segment thus forms the most stable element in the movement's thematic makeup. In thus reversing its former identity, the segment also reenacts and consolidates the relationship between the slow introduction of the movement, which is in the major, and the minor-mode movement proper. (This major-to-minor direction is distinctly unusual in music of the classical period.) The masculinity of the movement as a whole is thus framed, enveloped, potentiated, between feminine terms that set the boundaries of stability and instability.

At the same time, however, the music's masculine energy carries it outside this frame into outlying harmonic regions as the movement takes its course. And in the recapitulation of the second theme, the masculine segment has greater melodic stability than the feminine one because in the masculine the melodic line of the chorale is shared by the violin and piano for the first and only time. In the special interlude created by the second theme, then, masculine and feminine energies are genuinely complementary. Neither is complete without the other and neither can claim priority over the other, be it structural, expressive, or ideological. The second theme may form only a subordinate episode from one standpoint; from another it is an episode of magic.

The complex gendering of this theme has an interesting sequel. In 1923, Leoš Janáček wrote a string quartet later published as no. 1 and entitled "After Tolstoy's *Kreutzer Sonata*." The third of four movements begins with a canon between violin and cello, lyrical but edgy, as if between Pozdnyshev's wife and her imaginary lover; the first part of the canon is modeled closely on Beethoven's theme. On each of several statements, the canon meets with a brutal interruption; eventually the melody loses its canonic partner, becoming the voice of solitary desire, and the rhythm of melody and interruption becomes the essential business of the movement. According to Janáček, the quartet as a whole depicts "an unfortunate woman, suffering, beaten, ill-used, just as Tolstoy describes in his 'Kreutzer Sonata.'"[31] It is a work of profeminist, or at least profeminine, protest. It is also, however, a work of fantasy, a painfully ambivalent fantasy about feminine desire and antifeminine violence. The quartet was avowedly written out of Janáček's hopeless love for Kamila Stosslova, a married woman thirty-eight years his junior. The erotic lyricism and brutal interruptions of the "Beethoven" canon represent the composer's own desire and frustration over an infidelity that (much like Pozdnyshev's wife's) took place only in music.

Pole Star

As law, essence, or nature, gender polarity does nothing but harm. As metaphor, it can sometimes do good; it can offer figures, symbols, and narratives of the separate masculinities and femininities under whose wings most of us, at times, need to find shelter and solidarity. Doesn't every man, for instance, somewhere cherish a private narrative of how he won his masculinity by passing through an ordeal? There is a trace of this in my second wolf dream at the moment when the struggling bears are transformed, the moment when confusion yields to clarity and shapeless violence to the shape of desire. In the regime of gender polarity, a boy always achieves manhood by ordeal, by crossing a boundary at some cost to himself, while a girl achieves womanhood by "losing her virginity"—that is, by being defined as the past possessor of a boundary crossed and thereby established as both fact and value, by a man. The potential for oppressiveness in these cultural rituals is obvious. But does being obvious make the oppressiveness necessary in every case?

Whitman writes allegories of benign, because metaphorical, polarity in "The Sleepers." Think of the giant phallic swimmer: he can be vanquished only by the insensibility of the rocks, the hardness of a fate not personified or personifiable by a superego, even though the voyeuristic pleasure of his death panders to the superego. Later in the poem, Whitman describes an itinerant Native American woman with whom his mother, as a "nearly grown girl," fell in love:

> Never before had she seen such wonderful beauty and purity;
> She made her sit on a bench by the jamb of the
>   fireplace. . . . she cooked food for her,
> She had no work to give her but she gave her remembrance
>   and fondness.
>
> The red squaw staid all the forenoon, and toward the middle
>   of the afternoon she went away;
> O my mother was loth to have her go away.
>
> *ll. 119–23*

The native woman exemplifies pure femininity, without history, without further identity; she elicits pure nurturance, pure maternity, from Whitman's preadolescent mother-to-be. The rich maternity that his mother offers the poet is ultimately the native woman's gift, just as the paternity lost by the gigantic swimmer passes into the poet's poetic authority, represented by the solidified ink that replaces the giant's disseminated blood.

Both the swimmer and the "squaw" vanish without a trace. They live on only as figures, but as figures they live on and on. Their vanishing is what allows them to so do. Their vanishing into the figurative is what endows them with a beneficent gender polarity.

The Closet within the Closet

The obvious flaw in Whitman's erotic cosmos is the absence of lesbian desire; there is no feminine counterpart to manly love, "the dear love of man for his comrade, the attraction of friend to friend" ("The Base of All Metaphysics" l. 13). The omission is anything but unique to Whitman, but his disclosure of a possible motive for it may be unique in its candor.

Whitman associates desire for women with an uncontrollable, boundary-melting, all-confusing palpitation of male flesh:

> This is the female form . . .
> Mad filaments, ungovernable shoots play out of it, the
>   response likewise ungovernable,
> Hair, bosom, lips, bend of legs, negligent falling hands all
>   diffused, mine too diffused,
> Ebb stung by the flow and flow stung by the ebb, love-flesh
>   swelling and deliciously aching,
> Limitless limpid jets of love hot and enormous
> "I Sing the Body Electric" ll. 52, 57–60

This sort of response, this fleshly multiplication of erotic signs from mimicry to tumescence to ejaculation, is impossible to replicate on the female body, at least in acceptably phallomorphic terms, and Whitman seems to find desire for the female body inconceivable without it. A woman cannot desire another woman because she cannot show the signs, utter the chain of passwords, on her body. In turn, a man's desire for a woman can reach her only through that signifying chain. The man's heterosexual desire does not throw off certain fleshly signifiers as by-products; instead, the desire is the by-product thrown off by the signifiers. The tumult that attends this process, however, is so intense that the desiring body cannot endure it for long. (One might say that, for Whitman, there is no such thing as a premature ejaculation.) A key function of manly love is to quiet the tumult and to make it more endurable and enduring:

> Fast anchor'd eternal O love! O woman I love!
> O bride! O wife! more resistless than I can tell, the thought
>   of you!
> Then separate, as disembodied or another born,
> Etherial, the last athletic reality, my consolation,
> I ascend, I float in the regions of your love O man,
> O sharer of my roving life.
>   *"Fast Anchor'd Eternal O Love!"*

Nonetheless, there is one place in Whitman's poetry where lesbian desire does appear. It is the episode in "The Sleepers" about the poet's mother and the itinerant native woman:

My mother looked in delight and amazement at the stranger,
She looked at the beauty of her tallborne face and pliant
   limbs,
The more she looked upon her she loved her.

ll. 116–18

As the last section noted, the desire that the native woman
arouses is gratified through acts of tender caretaking. The intimate scene that results is the prototype for many others in which
Whitman finds eroticized pleasure in taking care of, feeling care
for, another man's body:

The runaway slave came to my house. . . .
[I] brought water and fill'd a tub for his sweated body and
   bruis'd feet,
And gave him a room that enter'd from my own

"Song of Myself" ll. 189, 193–94

The hurt and wounded I pacify with soothing hand. . . .
(Many a soldier's loving arms about this neck have cross'd
   and rested,
Many a soldier's kiss dwells on these bearded lips.)

"The Wound Dresser" ll. 61, 64–65

Like the native woman, too, the objects of loving manly care
often conjoin exquisite bodily "elasticity"—a combination of
beauty and sensitivity—with social lowliness or abjection. Whitman, it seems, learned how to love other men from his mother's
love for another woman.

Conquest of the Pole:

the masculine as magnetic north. It's almost the top of the world, the feminine south almost the bottom. The north-seeking compass needle is Pozdnyshev's dagger.

These are your instructions:

1. Discover you're at the pole already. Define the place where you stand as masculine by defining as feminine the place where you don't stand, didn't stand, couldn't stand, can't stand.

2. Secure this discovery by defining the feminine as that which cannot be inside you. When you find it inside you nonetheless, take pleasure in expelling it all at once: abject it, ejaculate it, cast it into an external feminine receptacle. (Caution: don't get merely hysterical, like Pozdnyshev. When you hurl the inkstand, stain your target. Make it signify you.) The feminine is that which gives pleasure in being expelled—more, that which takes pleasure in being expelled. Alternate version: receive the feminine as a foreign body, like a virus. It may give you a fever, even

pleasurably, but should also provoke the immune response that drives it away.

3. When you find the feminine inside you nonetheless, enjoy it in secret. Take pleasure in deferring the shame that would follow if your pleasure were discovered. Enjoy the sonata before you let it disgust you. Define the feminine as a precious recess, a hidden fold in yourself like a psychical vagina the lips of which you believe are sealed. Visit this place when no one, your superego included, can see you, but do so without quite admitting it; keep it secret even from yourself. That will let you face the world sincerely as all man. It will even let you believe in the magnetism of your own masculinity by letting you forget that magnetic north and true north are not the same.

Breaking Ranks

Nineteenth-century women were in on the secret that gender-polarized femininity is meant to hurt, and some of them found ways to say so. Elizabeth Barrett Browning's "A Musical Instrument" (1860) is virtually a parable of Oedipal subject-formation, the "making [of] a poet out of a man"—or woman—by the "great God Pan." Pan is described as hacking and hewing, cutting off short and pithing, a reed. This object of his creative violence is doubly allusive. On the one hand, it suggests the figure of Blaise Pascal's famous definition of human being, "Man is a thinking reed." On the other hand, it represents the metamorphosed Syrinx, the hapless nymph who vainly sought to escape Pan's clutches by becoming a reed, only to be made into the pipe that bears Pan's name, the musical instrument of the poem's title. Barrett Browning deliberately builds toward an acknowledgment of her own self-objectifying complicity in the cultural regime symbolized by Pan's authorized and authorizing sadism. She hails the music of the brutalized reed flute as "Sweet, sweet, sweet, O Pan! / Piercing sweet by the river! / Blinding sweet, O great god Pan!" (ll. 31–33). By seducing the ear, the piercingly sweet music blinds the eye to the violence that fathers such sweetness. The verse itself is seduced; its complex syncopated rhythms reproduce Pan's piping as helplessly as does the reed. But the poet resists. Only half-blind, she wrenches the poem to a close by chastising the brutal Pan as "half a beast" and claiming that the "true gods sigh for the cost and pain" of his cultural accomplishment. Somehow vaulting into a feminine position that sets polarity awry, Barrett Browning revoices Pan's music so that its sour notes ring true.

The great god Pan is the true god of gender polarity; he can only be full if something else is empty, only be all if something else is nothing:

> "This is the way," laughed the great god Pan
>> (Laughed while he sat by the river),
> "The only way, since gods began
> To make sweet music, they could succeed."
> Then, dropping his mouth to a hole in the reed.
>> He blew in power by the river.
>
> *ll. 25–30*

When he plays his enchanting pipe, Pan makes polarity look stable, but the canny listener (attuned to the voice of Syrinx) knows that this stability is a defensive illusion. The elements of living nature—the lilies and dragonflies of the river—that Pan both sweeps away with his violence and gathers back by his piping are indeterminate forms, one floating, one hovering, forms that pair without forming a binary, forms that conjoin without pairing. The polarity enforced by Pan's piping is only a means of masking a synergy that disperses gender into forms that belie all simple zero-sum games of masculine and feminine, m and n, a whole piece and the whole in pieces.

Odd Couples

The story is famous, of course: the invalid daughter of a tyrannical father becomes a famous poet, attracts the attentions of an ardent fellow-poet, and leaves her sickbed to flee with him to health and a new life in Italy. Before Robert Browning swept Elizabeth Barrett onto her feet, however, her spirits had been raised by Balzac and George Sand. Barrett Browning was troubled, though, by what she took to be Sand's virility, and she devoted a sonnet to the topic. This is from "To George Sand: A Recognition":

> dost deny
> The woman's nature with a manly scorn,
> And break away the gauds and armlets worn
> By weaker women in captivity?
> Ah! vain denial! that revolted cry
> Is sobbed in by a woman's voice forlorn, —
> Thy woman's hair, my sister, all unshorn

Floats back dishevelled strength in agony,
Disproving thy man's name.

ll. 1–9

The dangling gauds and clutching armlets unmask the normal condition of Western womanhood as one with that of a Turkish odalisque or, perhaps, of an Israelite slave girl in Egypt. The pleasure such women give, by both their ornamentation (hence their sexuality) and their servitude, is further identified with the agony proper to woman as a subject. That agony, in turn, takes material form as the woman's crowning glory, her unbound hair, an object of much fetishistic desire in the nineteenth century.

Barrett Browning is not only in on the secret that femininity is, and is meant to be, what hurts. She also knows that part of her willingly embraces the duty to dishevel her strength in agony. We might be tempted to dismiss this as a moral failure; the feminine protest against the great god Pan is undone here as the poet meekly kisses the rod. But Barrett Browning thinks that the moral failure is Sand's, not her own; it is just too easy to play a manly part. What is hard, what is heroic, is to wear one's feminine hurt as a badge of defiance. Wear the gauds, the armlets, and the hair at a certain angle, and the slave girl becomes a tyrant: Dalila, Turandot, Salome.

Depolarizing

Q: When is being straight really queer?

A: When it is an excuse to escape gender synergy.

Robert Browning, who tended to wax sentimental on the glories of heterosexual romance but is a marvelous chronicler of its disasters, caught sight of this one through the persona of the painter Andrea del Sarto. In the dramatic monologue that bears his name (1853), Andrea submits himself to a trio of masculine subject-figures—Leonardo, Raphael, and Michaelangelo—whom he perceives as accusatory. He perceives them, indeed, as classically castrating; they know that his paintings, though technically perfect, are lifeless. In response he develops a compensatory obsession with the proper drawing of bodies, which even leads him to correct an arm drawn by Raphael. It is conventional to blame Andrea's limpness on his adulterous wife Lucrezia, at once a ruthless phallic woman and the Renaissance version of a bimbo. But what if Lucrezia were only an excuse, a beard? What if Andrea needed the Oedipal defeat she provides in

order to flee from the shattering *jouissance* of an anti-Oedipal love
offered him by the "humane great monarch," Francis I:

> One finger in his beard or twisted curl
> Over his mouth's good mark that made the smile,
> One arm about my shoulder, round my neck,
> The jingle of his gold chain in my ear,
> I painting proudly with his breath on me.
>
> *ll. 154–58*

Francis's much-fingered beard projects an image of soft or yielding rather than phallic masculinity. Paternal in his authority,
Francis is maternal in his bearing, a source of both unlimited
approval and warm, diffuse oral-aural pleasure. He is, so to speak,
the woman that Barrett Browning's George Sand should have
become. Even more than Haroun Alraschid, Francis is the all-
loving father who knows nothing of guilt: the superego as the
breast. He offers Andrea a subjectivity without gender boundaries—and from this subjectivity, the perfect artist flees in abject
terror.

"Impassioned to the point of obscenity"

Why does Tolstoy need the trashy little piece, by who knows what composer, that is the real agent of seduction in "The Kreutzer Sonata"? Probably because he needs to be able to despise the music that has wrought such havoc and therefore needs something feminine. The "Kreutzer" Sonata itself is too overbearingly virile; even its "trite" second movement is too potent. No one feminizes Beethoven. (No one except Beethoven: but by tacit consensus this has gone unheard.[32]) An overwrought salon piece for violin and piano is the perfect object of contempt. Although for many years it was considered indecent for women to play the instrument, the violin in the nineteenth century, in a certain strain of throbbing lyricism, often represented feminine gracefulness, sentiment, or sensibility. Famous and once-famous examples include the "Scheherazade" theme from Rimsky-Korsakov's tone poem, the "Meditation" from Massenet's opera *Thaïs*, and Ernst's "Elegy" ("On the loss of a dear object"), which is also on the program at Pozdnyshev's salon. Even more to the point here, the violin in this vein could also suggest feminine desire, especially in figurative association with the female voice. In some cases such violin-voices were romantically coupled with masculine counterparts on cello (the young man's heart's lament, according to Whitman): in the Romance movement of Schumann's Fourth Symphony (oboe and cellos in the outer sections, solo violin in the middle section, the whole suggesting a portrait of the marriage of Robert and Clara Schumann in a work originally called the "Clara" Symphony); the Romance "Vois sous l'archet fremissant" (See beneath the quivering bow) from Offenbach's opera *Tales of Hoffmann* (solo cello and solo violin in lyric alternation, the voice that of a soprano in a trousers role); and the Nocturne of Borodin's Second String Quartet (solo cello and violin interchanging a melting melody at the emotional heart of a work dedicated to the composer's wife and written to commemorate the idyllic period of their first meeting). The violin-cello canon in Janáček's "Kreutzer Sonata" Quartet is a later version of the same trope. The feminine desire of the violin-voice is certainly at stake when Tolstoy's trashy piece is played by the effeminate Trukhachevski on behalf of Pozdnyshev's all too feminine wife. "I remember," says the husband, "her weak, piteous, and beatific smile as she wiped the perspiration from her flushed face when I came up to the piano" afterward (414).

The significance of these violin-voices appears, as if at a single bowstroke, in "Councillor Krespel; or The Cremona Violin," the story by E. T. A. Hoffmann that became the basis for the "Antonia" act in *Tales of Hoffmann*. Hoffmann's Antonia explicitly identifies her singing voice with the sound of a unique violin played by her father. The identification is a symbolic means of constraining her sexuality within the quasi-incestuous field of the father-daughter bond; when the father, in a dream or vision, sees and hears Antonia singing, what he observes is a lovedeath in which the intertwining of the violin-voice and piano assumes a patently sexual character: "He heard Antonia's voice singing softly and delicately until it grew into a shattering fortissimo. . . . He saw B- and Antonia embracing and gazing at each other rapturously. The notes of the song continued and the accompaniment of the piano continued, although Antonia was not visibly singing nor B- playing" (146). The outcome of this passion is Antonia's actual death, narratively from the consumption-like disease that gives her voice its magic, but symbolically from the excess of her sexual pleasure, or perhaps of his. In the father's fantasy, the climactic strain of the violin-voice is the daughter's orgasmic cry, which is a cry of separation from him that she is not permitted to survive. (She is not permitted to survive it even if, in fantasy, the lover is a cloak for the father himself.) The version by Offenbach and his librettist Jules Barbier adds a necromantic metafather, the evil Dr. Miracle, who denies Antonia to her actual father just as the father would deny her to her suitor. The result is a haunting image of the infinite regress of masculine authority. In the opera, Miracle orchestrates Antonia's fatal vocal ecstasy by visibly playing on a solo violin that we do not hear except insofar as it "sounds" imaginarily in Antonia's voice.

Hoffman's and Offenbach-Barbier's scenes form the extreme horizon of Tolstoy's. Unlike Antonia, Pozdnyshev's wife survives her violinistic orgasm very nicely; indeed, she thrives on it—it would never even occur to her to die of an orgasm, vocal or otherwise, which is one reason why her husband has to kill her.

Tolstoy's scene, in turn, forms a horizon for the lyrical effusions by solo violin I mentioned above, many of which are still popular, and more as well, from Beethoven's two Romances for violin and orchestra to the from-the-heart passages of Richard Rodney Bennett's symphonic arrangement of Jerome Kern's "Smoke Gets in Your Eyes." The quality of these pieces is unmistakable, a strange fusion of the bourgeois ideal of emotionally saturated femininity with a sexual overflow that the ideal seeks constantly to reabsorb. One might even suggest that the officially great solo violin concertos of the core repertoire, running from Beethoven to, say, Sibelius, are mainly concerned with appropriating the feminine vocality and sensitivity of the expressive solo violin to a masculine ideal. By integrating fervent lyricism and solistic display into a large-scale sonata-based structure, the concertos create a fantasy space in which the risk of castration does not exist. The voice of the era's violin concerto is that of a man of sensibility who is nonetheless truly manly. As Susan McClary says, the formal ideals of this musical tradition regularly depend on, and articulate, mastery over feminine expressivity.

Tolstoy probably did not know it, but Beethoven's "Kreutzer" Sonata is implicated in the sentimental passion of the fatal little piece, although the sonata does not contain anything of the sort itself. Recall that the finale of the sonata was taken over from another work. The first two movements of this earlier piece, the Sonata in A (Op. 30, no. 1), are sweetly lyrical, especially the second movement, Adagio molto espressivo, the melodies of which seek precisely the hyperfeminine lyricism that crosses into the zone of the female voice. This is true above all of the main theme, which, however, is a little nervous about its own emotional luxuriance; the theme is punctuated by curiously square and formal cadences, as if continually to give feminine fantasy an antidote of masculine self-control. The original finale, which we hear now in the "Kreutzer," is aggressive, percussive, and propulsive; its effect on the Sixth Sonata would be to disown the feminine fantasy with shocking roughness. Beethoven accordingly replaced it with a lyrical, rather subdued set of variations that, depending on how we are disposed to hear it, lets the fantasy stand or gives it a gentle corrective dose of formality and constraint. The joke is that, transferred to the "Kreutzer," the finale lacks enough weight to integrate the very large, highly contrastive movements that precede it; its manliness sounds like bravado. This revelation of masculinity as lack sets up an impulse toward femininity as surplus, or so we conclude from Tolstoy: after the "Kreutzer," one simply has to hear a little piece impassioned to the point of obscenity in order to release the eroticism that the great piece leaves pent up.

Erotoautism

Jacques Lantier, protagonist of Zola's novel *The Human Animal* (*La Bête humaine*), is an otherwise nice young man who wants above all things to kill a woman. Not that he dislikes women; not at all. He even dotes a bit on his foster mother and is half in love with his foster sister, Flore. But the closeness, touch, or laughter of a woman, above all the sight of an attractive woman's naked flesh, her breasts especially, make him want desperately to kill her. The woman he does eventually kill is someone he loves without reservation.

The passage in which Zola reveals Jacques's little quirk is one of the most horrifying in the literary canon, even by the callous standards of the late twentieth century. And even more horrifying than the content of this passage is the ease with which Zola, as narrator, slips into Jacques's mentality, the ease with which the authorial voice loses narrative distance in a pornographic intimacy of surging rhythmic prose and erotically charged visual detail. At one point the passage draws an analogy between "nor-

mal" males who dream from adolescence onward of "possessing" women and the aberrant Jacques, whose erotic dream has
always been of killing women. But this analogy collapses into an
identity in midst of the passage itself. It is as if there were no clear
line between the narrator's presumably normal masculinity and
Jacques's abnormal variant, just as there is no clear line between
a normal and a sadistic superego. Jacques himself, indeed, feels
driven by an imperative of primitive justice; he is a man charged
with avenging a prehistoric crime, "some malady with which
women had infected his race, [a] resentment passed down from
male to male since the first betrayal in the depths of some cave"
(67). But since Jacques is not, after all, the avenging superego
made flesh, but just a young man—rather gentle and polite than
otherwise—he is also conscience-stricken when he is not playing
scenes like the one that follows.

"Breast to breast" in a brutal clinch with Flore, who "longed
for him yet fought against him" (where have we heard this before?), Jacques accidentally-on-purpose exposes her torso:

> Her bodice was torn off and her breasts stood forth hard and
> swollen from the battle, milk-white in the pale night. Then
> she suddenly collapsed on her back, ready to give herself,
> defeated.
>
> But then, gasping for breath, instead of taking her he
> stopped and looked at her. Some madness seemed to be tak-
> ing possession of him. . . . He caught sight of [a] scissors
> gleaming in [a] heap of cord, and in a flash he picked them up
> and would have plunged them into the naked chest between
> the rose-tipped white breasts. But a sudden chill sobered him,
> and he threw down the scissors and ran away madly. . . . Kill a
> woman, kill a woman, that had buzzed through his ears since

his earliest adolescence with the increasing, all-powerful fervor of desire. As others, awakening into puberty, dream of
possessing a woman, so he was maddened by the vision of
killing one. For it was no use lying to himself, he had taken
up those scissors to plunge them into her flesh as soon as he
had seen that flesh, that warm and white breast. And it was
not because she was resisting him, oh no, it was for the enjoyment of it, because he wanted to and wanted to so badly that
if he were not clinging to the grass he would even now rush
back there and slit her open. (64–65)

The passage glamorizes the sexual violence it is supposed to
anatomize by confusing hatred of femininity with the ardor of
adolescent desire.

Even so, the passage does have an analytic, even a proto-
psychoanalytic, dimension. The details surrounding the recur-
rent image of Flore's breasts—their "milky" whiteness, their
swollenness, their nipples—clearly identify Jacques's sexual
arousal with a desire for oral, pre-Oedipal bliss. This bliss, however, is felt as castrating—the nipples are said to be hard, the
breasts swell up, phalluslike, during the struggle—because it belongs to the period that precedes the marking of sexual difference. Its fantasmatic enjoyment must therefore be followed at
once by the making visible of the polarity, phallic versus castrated, that establishes sexual difference. For Jacques, this means
both the marking of the positive, phallic pole, in his own arousal,
and (what is more often left implicit), the marking of the negative
pole by means of an open wound on the female body.

In the classical Freudian scenario, the male recoils at the sight
of the "wounded" female genitals and often denies feminine
"castration" (which prefigures his own) by redirecting his desire

to a fetish object. Jacques does this with the railway engine he is employed to drive, which he is repeatedly said to love as a man loves a mistress. But this is not enough. Jacques is compelled to re-mark the body of woman with the wound proper to it, to slit that body open, in order to render its negativity visible. Only by thus associating the sign of femininity with death can the sign of masculinity, the aroused penis misunderstood as the Lacanian phallus, be felt as the sign of life. By killing a woman, Jacques can suck at his own breast, invest his body with an organ that is at once a nipple, a penis, and a knife.

Differences

In the regime of gender polarity, the feminine is always one thing, the thing that hurts at the superego's pleasure. Nonetheless, femininity is not meant to hurt men and women in quite the same way. Neither men nor women can accept total submission to the superego; that would simply annihilate them as subjects. Not even the superego itself can function without a certain resistance; therefore a certain resistance is kindly permitted. Women, who embody femininity socially, must do so without wholly identifying with the femininity that they embody. (Part of Elizabeth Barrett Browning is lodged in George Sand.) Men, who dissemble femininity socially, must enact that femininity without at all identifying with it. (The great god Pan is "all" because he is all man.) In each case, there is a reserve of something in the subject beyond the feminine, and in each case this something is a position (or kernel) of nonidentification. In character, if not in quality or appearance, the reserve is the same for both sexes. Yet the difference between partial identification and nonidentification compels differing interpretations of this reserve. For men, the reserve is the sign that they do, after all, occupy the absolutely masculine position. For women, the reserve is the sign that they possess a "true" femininity outside the limits of (and therefore threatening to) gender polarity and its representations. These two interpretations, interpretations of the selfsame thing, combine both to set up the system of gender polarity and to define its inherent limitations.

Piece Work

Gender-polarized masculinity is supposed to culminate in the attainment of a profoundly inner-directed autonomy, unavailable to women because their femininity is, precisely, its lack. Yet this autonomy, this manhood, is always damaged by the means of its attainment; it is always conferred from a superior external position, and always on certain binding conditions. This manhood is supposed to be hard as a rock but is really a kind of geode: a dull ball of rock on the outside, a rich, complex crystal on the inside. The symmetry and beauty of the crystal can appear only if the rock is split in two. Sometimes the splitting cracks or disfigures what lies within as the cost of revealing it. And not all rocks that are capable of containing the crystal formation actually do contain it. Again, you can only tell when the rock is struck and split. The geode of manhood can present itself as intact only by coming asunder.

I count at least four ways, forming a complex array, in which this can happen.

Initiation. The aspirant to manhood crosses a threshold under the guidance or surveillance of someone, real or imaginary, who has crossed it before him. The crossing ends in the aspirant's "promotion" to masculine identity, or to a new level of that identity, but it also leaves behind a mark—a wound, scar, stigma, or insignia. This mark is the trace of a flaw that is displayed, and meant to be read, as a sign of wholeness.

Consider Pozdnyshev: he is initiated by being taken to a brothel. The experience introduces him to sexual knowledge and pleasure, but it also marks him permanently with self-contempt. "Sullied forever," his relationship to women becomes that of the alcoholic to a drink or a chain-smoker to a cigarette (367), and he shows the wound of that relationship daily in the twitchy compulsiveness of his own chain-smoking. Similarly, the frame narrator of "The Kreutzer Sonata" is initiated by his unwilled but unresisted complicity with Pozdnyshev's wife-murder. He consolidates his manhood by empathizing both with the other man's sexual violence and with its self-perpetuating mechanism of remorse and rationalization.

The examination. This is the negative form of initiation, in which the aspirant must "pass" the judgment of a hostile instructor whose approval is never better than grudging. Whitman frequently takes on the instructor's position when writing of manly love, perhaps as a means of warding off aspirants who would rather panic at male-male eroticism than welcome it:

> I give you fair warning before you attempt me further,
> I am not what you supposed, but far different....
> Your novitiate ... would be long and exhausting,

The whole past theory of your life and all conformity to the
    lives around you would have to be abandon'd,
Therefore release me now before troubling yourself any
    further, let go your hand from my shoulders,
Put me down and depart on your way
    "Whoever You Are Holding Me Now in Hand" ll. 3–4, 9–12

The examination reconfirms the necessity of masculine self-
alienation by identifying the instructor with an ideal self that the
aspirant can never become, but only strive to please. Hard to
please at best, this ideal self at worst deals out shame and humiliation with sadistic automatism. Whitman again:

O baffled, balk'd, bent to the very earth,
Oppress'd with myself that I have dared to open my mouth,
Aware now that amid all that blab whose echoes recoil upon
    me I have not once had the least idea who or what I am,
But that before all my arrogant poems the real Me yet stands
    untouch'd, untold, altogether unreach'd,
Withdrawn far, mocking me with mock-congratulatory signs
    and bows,
With peals of distant ironical laughter at every word I have
    written.
                    "As I Ebb'd" ll. 25–30

When Whitman glimpses the real Me, he sees himself through
the real Me's eyes, the eyes of the eternal schoolmaster. And what
he sees is not the true self he might yet become, but the false, the
fake, self he is perpetually condemned to be. The real Me is a
phantasm of the superego: a detached, censorious observer who
acts as a distorting mirror, stripping the narcissistic gloss from

the aspirant's language and thought and returning them to him in debased and debasing form.

The gift. Gender-polarized manhood sometimes comes as a spontaneous, inexplicable concession by the master or instructor. Whitman variously pictures himself as both the donor and the recipient of such a gift. As donor, he retrieves the calamus root from the depths of a secluded pond as from the waters or womb of life, and offers the root, which is phallic in shape, to his young male friends as a pledge or token ("These I Singing in Spring"). As recipient, he cherishes a branch of live oak he found in a simi- lar secluded recess, a similar virile womb, and twined round with moss to form a "curious token" of manly love ("I Saw in Louisi- ana a Live Oak Growing"). In each case, though, the gift is haunted by a faint sense of absence or futility. The calamus root must be given only to "them that love as I myself am capable of loving" (l. 28), but the Whitman who says this portrays himself as a solitary, surrounded only by phantoms, "a thick cloud of spirits" of "dear friends dead or alive" (ll. 24, 12). Likewise the sprig of live-oak is cherished only in silence and solitude as the poet speaks of his inability to live without "a friend a lover near" (l. 12).

Tennyson, too, places masculine identity in the economy of gift exchange. He sees Arthur Hallam as literally "gifted," a man whom "all the Muses / Deck'd with gifts of grace" (*85*, ll. 45– 46). These gifts are what make Hallam the male-maternal source of liquid speech and "a central warmth diffusing bliss" from which Tennyson gratefully receives similar gifts, albeit lesser ones. The recipient subject might be said to lose by this ex- change, which indelibly marks him as childlike and feminine. But Tennyson discounts all such loss as gain; he depicts the poverty that makes him a recipient as the source of donated wealth. The economic language is his own:

> He was rich where I was poor,
> And he supplied my want the more
> As his unlikeness fitted mine.
>
> *79, ll. 17–20*

No one gives charity to the rich. The gift is ultimately an act of grace, an undeserved concession; the giving thrives on the permanent unlikeness in worth between the master and the aspirant. At best, the aspirant can seek out traces of the master in himself, and thereby affirm himself. But the traces are no more than the fragmentary signs of a wholeness that can never be achieved:

> Whatever way my days decline,
> I felt and feel, tho' left alone,
> His being working in mine own,
> The footsteps of his life in mine.
>
> *86, ll. 41–44*

Emulation, imitation, identification: the aspirant poses these against his own implacable decline, and not without some success. But the path he follows is marked out only by signs of absence, the emptiness of the footsteps in which he follows without ever coming to fill their maker's shoes.

Theft. This is the negative of the gift, and, like the Promethean theft of fire, is always haunted by the prospect of guilt or shame. At best, one can have the theft condoned by the master: Tennyson's aspirant in "Recollections of the Arabian Nights" succeeds in that. He portrays himself as an intruder in the pleasure gardens of Haroun Alraschid, but an intruder who goes unpunished—not so much because he merits a triumph as because Haroun Alraschid punishes no one but instead welcomes anyone who can catch his merry, kindly, kingly gaze.

On other occasions, the theft is indeed supported by a fantasy of Oedipal triumph, but the fantasy is still furtive even in bravado. Whitman slips one such into "Song of Myself," tucking it away in the midst of a vast panorama of American scenes as if he were hoping to sneak it past us:

> I am a free companion, I bivouac by invading watchfires,
> I turn the bridegroom out of the bed and stay with the bride
>   myself,
> I tighten her all night to my thighs and lips.
>
> *"Song of Myself" ll. 817–19*

The watchfire adds a touch of Promethean energy, the wedding night a touch of ritual, as Whitman fantasizes seizing the bridegroom's position: the privileged and tireless position in which the phallic subject can conjoin the thighs of sexual pleasure with the lips of oracular power in the medium of the bride's compliant body. Neither myth nor ritual, however, can neutralize the violent subtext of this fantasy. Does the thief seize the phallus from the bridegroom by turning the bride's desire his own way? Or does he seize a phantasm that he mistakes for the phallus and proves on the bride's body by raping her?

The fantasy of theft may also inform the first movement of Beethoven's "Kreutzer" Sonata. This movement, it is important to remember, is set slightly askew. It is written in the key of A minor, but begins with a slow introduction in A major. This introduction falls into two parts, the first a stately display of rich sonorities, the second a quiet reflection on various aspects of a little two-note figure—a rising semitone with the accent on the second note. The movement "proper" begins when this little figure is, in effect, stolen on behalf of the minor key. The theft replaces the pairing of stateliness and reflectiveness with passionate, aggressive energy, and it converts the stolen little figure from a static warble into a fierce, pouncing gesture that becomes the dynamic source of many musical transformations (see example 2). The virile energy thus unleashed proves to be relentless, suspended only for the brief (but telling) episodes on the second theme and resumed thereafter with redoubled vigor. Yet the relentlessness is not quite unambiguous in its display of heroic "Homeric fighting." Its insistence has a defensive edge, as if even the slightest letup would signal a dangerous weakness and thereby open the door for a return to the more civilized, self-divided world of the introduction, where the empowering act of theft would be subject to reparation. Such a return almost happens just before the final bars of the movement, which, in turn, interdict the possibility of return with maximal energy and vehemence.

Initiation, examination, gift, theft: a complex array, but a consistent one. In each case, giving and withholding engage in a troubled negotiation that ends with a residue of discontent. The initiator gives, but never completely; the examiner withholds, but keeps promising to give. The results of initiation are idealized in the gift proper; the results of examination are exaggerated by theft.

Masculinity on terms like these is a virtual impossibility passed off as an actual necessity. No wonder, then, that it lashes out at all comers—though nothing in its frustrating predicament

Example 2. Beethoven, "Kreutzer" Sonata, first movement.
Transition from introduction to Presto.

can excuse its conduct. This masculinity is a rattletrap contraption that can't be fixed; it needs to be replaced. Can't someone figure out how to fire the superego? What if one were to leap the threshold, cut the exam, return the gift, disdain the theft? What if one chose not to break rocks like some member of a chain gang but rather to seek the glitter of crystal in the aspiring movements of air and water and light?

Holding It In

At a visceral level, misogyny expresses itself by identifying femininity with filth. Stray, formless matter, oozing liquids and the stains they leave behind, become both the signs that betray the true character of the feminine and the traces that women accordingly seek to cover or erase. The feminine is that which has to be cleaned up. If necessary, it has to be scoured. The anal zone in particular, which "normal" socialization stigmatizes as abject, vile, repellent, becomes subject to a migration and expansion that can make it seem the secret locus of femininity. Lou Andreas-Salome, in her role as early psychoanalyst, even goes so far as to say that, psychologically, the vagina as container and passageway is taken "on loan" from the anus. In eighteenth-century satire, the surest way to demystify the charm or degrade the intellect of women is to discover their link to the paint-pot and the chamberpot. In this passage from Pope, "Rufa" is a typical redhead, thought to be lascivious, and "Sappho" is Lady Mary Wortley Montagu, from whom we have already heard:

Rufa, whose eye quick glancing oe'r the Park,
Attracts each light gay meteor of a Spark,
Agrees as ill with Rufa studying Locke,
As Sappho's diamonds with her dirty smock,
Or Sappho at her toilet's greazy task,
With Sappho fragrant at an ev'ning Mask:
So morning Insects that in muck begun,
Shine, buzz, and fly-blow in the setting-sun.
  "Of the Characters of Women" ll. 21–28

In nineteenth-century iconography, femininity and feminine sexuality are linked to a supposed overdevelopment of the buttocks, a trait thought to be atavistic and made famous in the especially hypertrophied form associated with Hottentot women.[33] The outsize buttocks also signify outsize labia, which they make visible in displaced form; as Sander Gilman and Richard Leppert both note, the buttocks and labia of Saartje Bartmann, the nineteenth-century "Hottentot Venus," were still on display in Paris in the 1990s. (They have only recently been removed.) As we know, Trukhachevski is marked by this particular stigma, which reveals both his femininity and his musicality. In fact, our last glimpse of him in "The Kreutzer Sonata" is from behind, as, in flight from the dagger-wielding Pozdnyshev, he darts under the piano and out the door.

This excremental pattern may help to explain the characteristic interlock of brutality and apology in sexual violence. The violence produces its own stigmata of blood and bruises; that's the way it looks when you beat the shit out of someone. Rage takes pleasure in the sight, but when rage has cooled, the sight induces shame. *I'm so sorry, I feel terrible, I'll never do it again* is the formula for shame. It is a formula that applies with unsettling ease to both beating a woman and soiling one's pants.

At the Crossroads

Don't believe Oedipus when he says that it wasn't his fault, that he just stumbled into parricide and incest while trying to avoid them. Oedipus was looking for trouble; he didn't care what kind. At some point Oedipal masculinity inevitably looks for trouble.

One way that gender polarity defines masculinity is as complete mastery over all feminine positions. Such mastery is necessarily imaginary but that fact does not necessarily work to its detriment; social reality is often just the sum of fantasy and power. Any fantasy requires a nugget of resistant reality in order to feel credible, to be something more than just a fantasy. Masculinity seeks that nugget in feminine resistance, which it turns to pleasure by surmounting, often with ritualized, sometimes with real violence. To be sure, sexual violence is partly the product of the actual instability of gender polarity. This whole book has insisted on the point. But sexual violence is also, perhaps even more damagingly, a product of a staged, fictitious instability, the aim of which is to enforce and reinforce what only appears to be buckling. The business of the manly enforcer is dalliance with violence, and this business is his pleasure.

It follows, pleasure being the most invulnerable of enemies, that sociologically inspired means for curing society of sexual violence—better masculine role models, disengagement of violence from sex and glamour in the media, the cultivation of sensitivity—will mostly prove straws in the wind. What has to be changed is the psychodynamics of gender. What has to be changed is the symbolic order itself. We need a new unconscious. Much that once seemed right and natural must come to seem toxic; much that used to make us queasy must come to give unforced pleasure.

How can such a thing happen? How can we foster it? Well, one enduring legacy of psychoanalysis, even for those who resist many of its tenets, is an awareness of the depth at which habits of fantasy shape the subject, or are even shaped into the subject. If we could change those habits, we might find sexual violence becoming harder to imagine, and so, in the long run, harder to commit. The trouble here is that overt, tendentious changes will be of little use; we can tell the right stories and say the right things and still do little more than reinforce our virtuous self-regard. Change must somehow occur precisely at the subtextual levels where we ordinarily have little control. Perhaps we can court that change by seeking to place ourselves in situations, real or imaginary, where we fail to maintain our usual subject-positions and find that we not only do not suffer from this failure but enjoy it. Going further, we can seek to loosen what now pass as rational constraints on the relation of fantasy and identity, or more exactly on the subordination of fantasy to identity. If we could glide from one subject-position to another with some of Walt Whitman's eroticized fluidity and ecumenical curiosity, we might be less inclined to fortify and fetishize a single privileged or proper position. As a reader, listener, or spectator, I can identify with the position of any imaginary subject no matter how unlike me that subject is. But I do not thereby delude myself that I am that subject. Why should I entertain that delusion by naively identifying with the "real" subject I imagine myself to be? I can be any of Whitman's twenty-nine bathers, who can be of any sex, any gender. There is no self to stand like a breakwater between land and sea, only one that continually desolidifies, undulating like the shoreline under the moving fingers of wind and water.

This is not to say, however, that we can naively expect gender polarity to wither away. It is too compelling on many grounds, laden with fantasies, pleasures, and narrative incitements that are hard to escape no matter how clearly we recognize its pathologies. Besides, its sheer historical weight is overwhelming; the fact that children enact polarized gender roles whether they are supposed to or not has become an item of folklore among parents who would rather they didn't. What we can expect, rather, is to undo the self-mystified dominance of gender polarity, its fear of reversal and reprisal, its queasiness at gender synergy, its homophobia, its deadly earnestness. We can reconfigure polarity so that it is no longer the norm from which synergy deviates but one (or one group) of the outcomes of synergy itself. The persistence of polarity tells us that we need and want, like it or not, to act as if gender and sexuality had true, transcendental natures. The emergence of synergy tells us that we need and want to recognize that such natures are not to be had. What we need as well, but have not yet wanted enough, is to understand that this contradiction is the source, not only of the terrors and deformities of gender and sexuality, but also of their pleasure, their variety, their power, their wonder.

The White Wolf

of my second wolf dream replaces a deed of sexual violence—the primal scene too violent to be seen and therefore X'd out, scribbled over until all that remains is an opaque, shapeless mass—with a blissful apparition in which gender positions intermingle. White on white: against the snow, the wolf springs forth like the snow itself spun by the wind, a figure whose outline can be seen but not fixed, the text of a tale yet to be written across the blank page. The wolf is a phantom, but not a remnant or revenant: it is the originary phantom from which the whole dream scene derives and to which, after having produced it, the whole scene tends. . . . I wish you could see my wolf; you would like his tensile grace, her constellated shimmer of gender synergy. I can't tell you how strange and how good it is to be a beautiful white wolf treading lightly on the light snow. . . .

Notes

1. See Mitchell, de Lauretis, and Brennan (emphasis on Freud); Irigaray, Gallop, and Silverman (emphasis on Lacan).

2. The anti-Freudian revival was spurred by Masson, theorized by Grünbaum, and popularized by Crews.

3. For such critiques, see Robinson and Cavell.

4. For a sympathetic critique of the overvaluation of gender-bending and -blending, see Martin.

5. On the interrelations of modernism, gender, and sexuality see Gubar and Gilbert (misogyny), Sedgwick (homophobia), and Huyssen.

6. Whitman, "By Blue Ontario's Shore (1856 version), l. 159; Goethe, quoted by O. Sacks, p. 232.

7. Chodorow's sociologically oriented approach has been influential; Kofman and Sprengnether offer approaches based on rigorous readings of Freud.

8. This is de Lauretis's argument in "Desire and Narrative."

9. Silverman, *Masculine Subjectivity* 185–214; Lacan, "Subversion" 316–25.

10. Laplanche theorizes the shift from bodily need to fantasy on the basis of a reading of Freud in *Life and Death*.

11. For detailed discussion, see Butler, "Lesbian Phallus," and Silverman, "Lacanian Phallus."

12. For a critique of this confusion based on readings of Plato and Freud, see Irigaray, *Speculum.*

13. Freud, *Ego* 24; Silverman, *Masculine Subjectivity* 191–95.

14. On the paradoxical nature of this mirage, see Žižek, *Tarrying* 35–39, which also offers a more detailed discussion of The Thing and its prefiguration in the work of Kant.

15. On gender and genius, see Battersby.

16. On this process of feminization see Christ; also Kramer, "Salome."

17. Dellamora 16–41.

18. Although *In Memoriam* was published after *The Princess,* most of it was written earlier.

19. Plato, *Ion* 18–19.

20. On "gender trouble"—term and concept—see Butler.

21. On the glass closet, see Sedgwick, *Epistemology* 221–230.

22. For more on this aspect of musicality, see my *Classical/Postmodern* 33–66.

23. On Madonna's mimicry of Jackson, see Garber 118–27.

24. See Dinerstein and Chodorow.

25. The concept is Nicolas Abraham's; see Abraham and Torok.

26. On the value of classical sculpture in aestheticist and homosexual subcultures, see Dellamora 102–16.

27. For a synoptic account, see Halperin.

28. For more on Beethoven's *Coriolan* in this context see my "Strange Case."

29. For a trenchant critique of "hormonal" explanations (involving an essentialized "male sadism") see Clover, "The Eye of Horror" 214–25.

30. On "the wish to be woman"—term and concept—see de Courtivron.

31. Quotation from *Leoš Janáček*, a catalog of published works (Prague: Artia, 1959), 33.

32. Susan McClary, however, has told both sides of this story. See *Feminine Endings* 68–69, 126–31, for the masculine half; "Pitches, Expression, Ideology" for the feminine.

33. For the history of this association, see Gilman.

Bibliography

Nicholas Abraham. "Notules sur le fantôme." *L'Écorce et le noyeau*. By Abraham, with Maria Torok. Paris: Aubier-Flammarion, 1978.

Lou Andreas-Salome. "'Anal' und 'Sexual.'" *Imago* 4 (1916): 249.

Mikhail Bakhtin. *Rabelais and His World*. Trans. Hélène Iswolksy. Cambridge, Massachusetts: MIT Press, 1968.

Christine Battersby. *Gender and Genius: Towards a Feminist Aesthetics*. Bloomington: University of Indiana Press, 1989.

Charles Baudelaire. *Paris Spleen*. Trans. Louise Varese. New York: New Directions, 1947.

Teresa Brennan. *The Interpretation of the Flesh: Freud and Femininity*. New York: Routledge, 1992.

Elizabeth Barrett Browning. *Sonnets from the Portuguese and Other Poems*. New York: Dover, 1992.

Robert Browning. *The Shorter Poems of Robert Browning*. Ed. William C. Devane. New York: Appleton-Century-Crofts, 1934.

Judith Butler. *Gender Trouble: Feminism and the Subversion of Identity*. New York: Routledge, 1990.

———. "The Lesbian Phallus and the Morphological Imaginary." *Differences* 6 (1992) ("The Phallus Issue"): 133–71.

Marcia Cavell. *The Psychoanalytic Mind: From Freud to Philosophy.* Cambridge, Massachusetts: Harvard University Press, 1993.

Anton Chekhov. "The Lady with the Pet Dog." Trans. and ed. Avrahm Yarmolinksy. *The Portable Chekhov.* New York: Viking Press, 1947.

Nancy Chodorow. *The Reproduction of Mothering: Psychoanalysis and the Sociology of Gender.* Berkeley: University of California Press, 1978.

Carol Christ. "The Feminine Subject in Victorian Poetry." *ELH: A Journal of English Literary History* 54 (1987): 385–402.

Catherine Clément. *Opera; or, the Undoing of Women.* Trans. Betsey Wing. Minneapolis: University of Minnesota Press, 1988.

Carol Clover. "The Eye of Horror." *Viewing Positions: Ways of Seeing Film.* Ed. Linda Williams. New Brunswick: Rutgers University Press, 1994. 184–230.

Samuel Taylor Coleridge. *Poems.* Ed. John Beer. London: Dent, 1974.

Isabelle de Courtivron. "Weak Men and Fatal Women." *Homosexuality and French Literature.* Ed. George Stamboulian and Elaine Marks. Ithaca: Cornell University Press, 1979. 210–27.

Frederick Crews. "The Unknown Freud." *New York Review of Books* 41 (November 18, 1993): 55–66.

———. "'The Unknown Freud': An Exchange." *New York Review of Books* 41 (February 3, 1994): 55–60.

Teresa de Lauretis. "Desire in Narrative." *Alice Doesn't: Feminism, Semiotics, Cinema.* Bloomington: University of Indiana Press, 1984. 103–57.

———. "Habit Changes." *Differences: A Journal of Feminist Cultural Studies* 6 (1994): 296–313.

———. *The Practice of Love: Lesbian Sexuality and Perverse Desire.* Bloomington: University of Indiana Press, 1994.

Gilles Deleuze and Felix Guattari. *Anti-Oedipus: Capitalism and Schizophrenia.* Trans. Robert Hurley, Mark Seem, and Helen R. Lang. New York: Viking, 1977.

Richard Dellamora. *Masculine Desire: The Sexual Politics of Victorian Aestheticism.* Chapel Hill: University of North Carolina Press, 1990.

Bram Dijkstra. *Idols of Perversity: Fantasies of Feminine Evil in Fin-de-Siècle Culture.* New York: Oxford University Press, 1988.

Dorothy Dinerstein. *The Mermaid and the Minotaur: Sexual Arrangements and Human Malaise.* New York: Harper and Row, 1976.

Mary Ann Doane. "Film and the Masquerade: Theorizing the Female Spectator." *Femmes Fatales: Feminism, Film Theory, Psychoanalysis.* New York: Routledge, 1991. 17–32.

T. S. Eliot. *Collected Poems: 1909–1962.* New York: Harcourt, Brace, and World, 1963.

Ekbert Faas. *Retreat into the Mind: Victorian Poetry and the Rise of Psychiatry.* Princeton: Princeton University Press, 1988.

Michel Foucault. *The History of Sexuality, Volume I: An Introduction.* Trans. Robert Hurley. New York: Random House, 1978.

Sigmund Freud. "'Civilized' Sexual Morality and Modern Nervousness" (1908). *Standard Edition* 9: 179–204. Cited from Freud, *Sexuality and the Psychology of Love.* Ed. Philip Rieff. New York: Macmillan, 1963.

———. "Dostoyevsky and Parricide" (1928). *Standard Edition* 21: 177–94. Cited from Freud, *Character and Culture.* Ed. Philip Rieff. Macmillan: New York, 1963.

———. "The Economic Problem of Masochism" (1924). *Standard Edition* 19: 159–70.

———. *The Ego and the Id* (1923). *Standard Edition* 19: 1–66. Cited from Freud, *The Ego and the Id.* Ed. James Strachey. New York: W. W. Norton, 1965.

———. "Family Romances" (1908). *Standard Edition* 9: 237–41.

———. *From the History of an Infantile Neurosis* ("The Wolf Man" 1918). *Standard Edition* 17: 1–124. Cited from Freud, *Three Case Histories.* New York: Macmillan, 1963. 187–319.

———. "The Most Prevalent Form of Degradation in Erotic Life" (1912). *Standard Edition* 11: 179–90, under the title "On the Universal Tendency to Debasement in the Sphere of Love." Cited from Freud, *Sexuality and the Psychology of Love.* Ed. Philip Rieff. New York: Macmillan, 1963.

———. *The Psychopathology of Everyday Life* (1901). *Standard Edition* 6. Cited from Freud, *The Psychopathology of Everyday Life*. Ed. James Strachey. New York: W. W. Norton, 1965.

———. "Screen Memories" (1899). *Standard Edition* 3: 299–322.

———. *The Standard Edition of the Complete Psychological Works of Sigmund Freud*, 24 volumes. Trans. and ed. James Strachey. London: Hogarth Press, 1953–1973.

Jane Gallop. *The Daughter's Seduction: Feminism and Psychoanalysis.* Ithaca: Cornell University Press, 1982.

———. *Reading Lacan.* Ithaca: Cornell University Press, 1985.

Marjorie Garber. *Vested Interests: Cross-Dressing and Cultural Anxiety.* New York: Routledge, 1992.

Paul Gauguin. *Noa Noa.* Ed. Pierre Petit. Paris: Jean-Jacques Pauvert, 1988.

Sander Gilman. "Black Bodies, White Bodies: Toward an Iconography of Female Sexuality in Late Nineteenth-Century Art, Medicine, and Literature." *Critical Inquiry* 12 (1985): 204–42.

Adolph Grünbaum. *Foundations of Psychoanalysis.* Berkeley: University of California Press, 1984.

Susan Gubar and Sandra Gilbert. *No Man's Land: The Place of the Woman Writer in the Twentieth Century.* New Haven: Yale University Press, 1988.

David M. Halperin. "Sex Before Sexuality: Pederasty, Power, and Politics in Classical Athens." *Hidden from History: Reclaiming the Gay and Lesbian Past.* Ed. Martin Baumal Duberman, Martha Vicinus, and George Chauncey, Jr. New York: New American Library, 1989. 37–53.

James Hepokoski. "Masculine/Feminine." *Musical Times* 135 (1994): 494. Translation cited has been slightly modified.

E. T. A. Hoffmann. *Tales.* Ed. and trans. Leonard J. Kent and Elizabeth C. Knight. Chicago: University of Chicago Press, 1969.

Andreas Huyssen. *After the Great Divide: Modernism, Mass Culture, Postmodernism.* Bloomington: University of Indiana Press, 1986.

Luce Irigaray. *Speculum of the Other Woman.* Trans. Gillian C. Gill. Ithaca: Cornell University Press, 1985.

———. *This Sex Which Is Not One.* Trans. Catherine Porter with Carolyn Burke. Ithaca: Cornell University Press, 1985.

Franz Kafka. *Complete Stories.* Ed. Nahum Glatzer. New York: Schocken, 1971.

Sara Kofman. *The Enigma of Woman: Woman in Freud's Writings.* Ithaca: Cornell University Press, 1985.

Lawrence Kramer. *Classical Music and Postmodern Knowledge.* Berkeley: University of California Press, 1995.

———. "Music and Cultural Hermeneutics: The Salome Complex." *Cambridge Opera Journal* 2 (1990): 269–94.

———. *Music and Poetry: The Nineteenth Century and After.* Berkeley: University of California Press, 1984.

———. "The Strange Case of Beethoven's *Coriolan:* Romantic Aesthetics, Modern Subjectivity, and the Cult of Shakespeare." *Musical Quarterly* 79 (1995): 256–80.

Julia Kristeva. *Revolution in Poetic Language.* Trans. Margaret Waller. New York: Columbia University Press, 1984.

Jacques Lacan. "The Signification of the Phallus." *Écrits: A Selection.* Trans. Alan Sheridan. New York: W. W. Norton, 1977. 282–91.

———. "The Subversion of the Subject and the Dialectic of Desire in the Freudian Unconscious." *Écrits: A Selection.* Trans. Alan Sheridan. New York: W. W. Norton, 1977. 292–325.

Jean Laplanche. *Life and Death in Psychoanalysis.* Trans. Jeffrey Mehlman. Baltimore: Johns Hopkins University Press, 1976.

———. *New Foundations for Psychoanalysis.* Trans. David Macey. Oxford: Basil Blackwell, 1989.

Richard Leppert. *The Sight of Sound: Music, Representation, and the History of the Body.* Berkeley: University of California Press, 1993.

Eric Lott. *Love and Theft: Blackface Minstrelsy and the American Working Class.* New York: Oxford University Press, 1993.

Catharine MacKinnon. *Only Words.* Cambridge, Massachusetts: Harvard University Press, 1993.

Biddy Martin. "Extraordinary Homosexuals and the Fear of Being Ordinary." *Differences* 6 (1994): 100–125.

A. B. Marx. *Die Lehre von der musikalische Komposition.* 2nd ed. Leipzig: 1845. Quoted in Hepokoski.

Jeffrey Moussaieff Masson. *The Assault on Truth: Freud's Suppression of the Seduction Theory.* New York: Farrar, Straus, and Giroux: 1984.

Juliet Flower McCannell. *The Regime of the Brother: After the Patriarchy.* New York: Routledge, 1991.

Susan McClary. *Feminine Endings: Music, Gender, and Sexuality.* Minneapolis: University of Minnesota Press, 1991.

———. "Pitches, Expression, Ideology: An Exercise in Mediation." *Enclitic* 7 (1983): 76–86.

Daphne Merkin. "Unlikely Obsession." *The New Yorker*, February 26 and March 4, 1996: 98–115.

Juliet Mitchell. *Psychoanalysis and Feminism.* New York: Viking, 1974.

Lady Mary Wortley Montagu. "Epistle from Mrs. Yonge to Her Husband." *Essays and Poems and Simplicity, a Comedy.* Ed. Robert Halsband and Isobel Grundy. London, 1977.

Laura Mulvey. "Visual Pleasure and Narrative Cinema." *Visual and Other Pleasures.* Bloomington: University of Indiana Press, 1989. 14–26.

Thomas Nagel. "Freud's Permanent Revolution." *New York Review of Books* 41 (May 12, 1994): 34–38.

Friedrich Nietzsche. *The Gay Science.* Trans. Walter Kaufman. New York: Random House, 1974.

Plato. *Ion. Great Dialogues of Plato.* Trans. W. H. D. Rouse. New York: New American Library, 1956.

Alexander Pope. "On the Characters of Women." *Poems of Alexander Pope.* Ed. John Butts. New Haven: Yale University Press, 1963.

Ellie Raglund-Sullivan. *Jacques Lacan and the Philosophy of Psychoanalysis.* Urbana: University of Illinois Press, 1987.

Paul Robinson. *Freud and His Critics*. Berkeley: University of California Press, 1994.

Charles Rosen. *The Classical Style: Haydn, Mozart, Beethoven*. New York: Viking, 1971.

Oliver Sacks. *Awakenings*. New York: HarperCollins, 1973.

———. *The Man Who Mistook His Wife for a Hat, and Other Clinical Tales*. New York: Simon and Schuster, 1985.

Peter Sacks. *The English Elegy: Studies in the Genre from Shakespeare to Yeats*. Baltimore: Johns Hopkins University Press, 1985.

Daniel Paul Schreber. *Memoirs of My Nervous Illness*. Trans. Ida Macalpine and Richard A. Hunter. Cambridge, Massachusetts: Harvard University Press, 1988.

Robert Schumann. *On Music and Musicians*. Ed. Konrad Wolff. Trans. Paul Rosenfeld. New York: W. W. Norton, 1946.

Eve Kosofsky Sedgwick. *Between Men: English Fiction and Male Homosocial Desire*. New York: Columbia University Press, 1988.

———. *Epistemology of the Closet*. Berkeley: University of California Press, 1990.

William Shakespeare. *The Complete Works*. Ed. Alfred Harbage. Baltimore: Penguin, 1969.

Kaja Silverman. "The Lacanian Phallus." *Differences* 6 (1992) ("The Phallus Issue"): 84–115.

———. *Masculine Subjectivity at the Margins*. New York: Routledge, 1992.

Madelon Sprengnether. *The Spectral Mother: Freud, Feminism, and Psychoanalysis*. Ithaca: Cornell University Press, 1990.

Wallace Stevens. *The Collected Poems of Wallace Stevens*. New York: Alfred A. Knopf, 1954.

August Strindberg. *Creditors. Pre-Inferno Plays*. Trans. Walter Johnson. New York: W. W. Norton, 1970.

Alfred Lord Tennyson. *Poems of Tennyson*. Ed. Jerome Buckley. Boston: Houghton Mifflin, 1958.

Leo Tolstoy. "The Kreutzer Sonata." Trans. Louise and Aylmer Maude. *Great Short Works of Tolstoy.* New York: Harper and Row, 1967.

Donald Francis Tovey. *A Companion to Beethoven's Pianoforte Sonatas.* London: Associated Boards of the R. A. M. and R. C. M., 1931.

Walt Whitman. *Leaves of Grass.* Ed. Sculley Bradley and Harold W. Blodgett. New York: W. W. Norton, 1973.

Oscar Wilde. "The Ballad of Reading Gaol." *The Complete Works of Oscar Wilde.* Ed. J. B. Foreman. London, 1966.

Forbes Winslow. Extract from the *Journal of Psychological Medicine* 2 (1849): 262. Quoted by Faas.

William Wordsworth. *The Oxford Authors: William Wordsworth.* Ed. Stephen Gill. Oxford: Oxford University Press, 1984.

Slavoj Žižek. *Looking Awry: An Introduction to Jacques Lacan through Popular Culture.* Cambridge, Massachusetts: MIT Press, 1992.

———. *Tarrying with the Negative: Kant, Hegel, and the Critique of Ideology.* Durham, North Carolina: Duke University Press, 1993.

Émile Zola. *La Bête humaine.* Trans. Leonard Tancock. Harmondsworth, Middlesex: Penguin, 1977.

———. *Thérèse Raquin.* Trans. Leonard Tancock. Harmondsworth, Middlesex: Penguin, 1962.

Index

I would like to thank Claire Leonard for her help in preparing this index—and for the pertinent question she added to her list of references to the various Kreutzer sonatas, "Does anyone know what music really is?"

abjection, 87–89
Alboni, Marietta, 58–59
anality, 108–9, 260
Andreas-Salome, Lou, 259
anti-Oedipal relations, 53–54, 184
  and *passim*

Bacchus, 62–63
Bakhtin, Mikhail, 163
Bartmann, Saartje, 260
Baudelaire, Charles, 62–64
Beethoven, Ludwig van, 4–5, 18,
  20; *Coriolan*, 143–44; "Kreutzer"
  Sonata (violin and piano), first
  movement, 44–45, 79–80, 82–
  83, 108, 113, 201–2, 215–23,
  254–55; "Kreutzer" Sonata, sec-
  ond movement, 81–84, 111–12,
  113; "Kreutzer" Sonata, finale,
83–84, 241–42; Piano Sonatas
  Op. 57 ("Appassionata") and 111,
  84; Sonata for Violin and Piano
  in A (Op. 30, no. 1), 241–42
Bellini, Vincenzo, 55–57
Bennett, Richard Rodney, 241
Berlioz, Hector, 61
Bernstein, Leonard, 111
Bobbitt, Lorena (and John Wayne),
  18, 180, 183
Borodin, Alexander, String Quartet No. 2, 239
Browning, Elizabeth Barrett, 247;
  "A Musical Instrument," 231–
  33; "To George Sand," 234–35
Browning, Robert: "Andrea del
  Sarto," 236–37; "By the Fire-
  side," 191–92; "Two in the
  Campagna," 178

Call of the Wild, The (London), 47–48
Carmen (Bizet), 123
castration, 7, 96, 99–100, 101–4, 164, 167, 183, 203, 245–46
Chekhov, Anton, 103
Clément, Catherine, 55, 57, 123, 125
Coleridge, Samuel Taylor, 30–32, 72–73, 96
Concert Singer, The (Eakins) 129, *130*, 131
"Cremona Violin, The" (Hoffmann), 239–40

da Vinci, Leonardo, 161
Death in Venice (Mann), 142
de Lauretis, Teresa, 9
Debussy, Claude, 111
Deleuze, Gilles, 21
Dinerstein, Dorothy, 17
Doane, Mary Ann, 131
Don Giovanni (W. A. Mozart), 211
Donizetti, Gaetano, *Lucia di Lammermoor* and *La Favorita*, 55–57
Dostoyevsky, Fyodor, 24–26

Eakins, Thomas, 129–31
ego ideal, 97
Eliot, T. S., 1, 171
Enlightenment, 177–79
erotic desire, 185–88
examination, and masculine identity, 250–52

family romance (Freud), 52
feminist psychoanalysis, 119–22
fetishism, 78, 95, 129–31, 172, 245–46
Flying Dutchman, 32

Foucault, Michel, 15
Freud, Sigmund, 9, 41, 49, 90, 186 and *passim;* "'Civilized' Sexual Morality," 22; "Dostoyevsky and Parricide," 24–26; *The Ego and the Id*, 22–24, 76; *The Psychopathology of Everyday Life*, 38–39

Gauguin, Paul, 164, 168
gaze, 42–43, 129–31, 182, 184–85
gender polarity, 10–12, 224–25, 229 and *passim*
gender synergy, 12–15, 60, 261–63 and *passim*
genital proviso, 198–200
Gentlemen Prefer Blondes (Howard Hawks), 174–76
gift, and masculine identity, 252–53
Gilman, Sander, 260
Goethe, Johann Wolfgang von, 19
Goya, Francisco, 29
Guattari, Félix, 21

Hawks, Howard, 174
Hildegard of Bingen, 155–57
Hoffmann, E. T. A., 239–40
homophobia, 17, 170, 197–200
homosociality, 197, 201–2
hysteria, 126, 156, 214

imaginary order (Lacan), 28, 42
initiation, and masculine identity, 250
Irigaray, Luce, 29

Jackson, Michael, 111
Janáček, Leos, String Quartet No. 1, "After Tolstoy's *Kreutzer Sonata*," 222–23, 239
jealousy, 208–9

jouissance, 27, 54, 88, 108, 111, 123, 135, 163, 185, 193

Kafka, Franz, 173–74
Kern, Jerome, 241
Kramer, Lawrence, dreams. *See* Wolf dreams
Kristeva, Julia, 53

Lacan, Jacques, 6, 8, 23, 27–28, 41–43, 110, 132, 163
lack, 104, 132–33, 211–12
"Lady with the Pet Dog, The" (Chekhov), 103
Laplanche, Jean, 153, 186
Leppert, Richard, 77, 129, 202, 260
lesbian desire, 226–29
Liszt, Franz, 62–63
London, Jack, 47–48
lovedeath, 134–40, 150

MacKinnon, Catharine, 204
Madonna, 111
Mallarmé, Stephane, 111
Mann, Thomas, 142
Marx, A. B., 216
masochism, 150
Massenet, Jules, "Meditation" from *Thaïs*, 238
McCannell, Juliet Flower, 177
McClary, Susan, 216, 241
Medusa, 102–3, 185
Merkin, Daphne, 187
minstrelsy, 159–60
misogyny, 177–79
Monroe, Marilyn, 174–76, 182
Montagu, Lady Mary Wortley, 206–7, 259–60
Mulvey, Laura, 123

music, 44–45, 60, 78–80, 108–12, 129–31, 171–72, 213–14 and *passim*. *See also* Opera; Piano; Violin

Nagel, Thomas, 8–9
narrative, 30–33, 96, 146, 224
necrophilia, 194–96
Nietzsche, Friedrich, 178–79
Nijinsky, Vaslav, 111
Norma (Bellini), 55–57

Odysseus, 173–76
Oedipal relations, 21–26, 52, 65–76, 136–38, 169, 261 and *passim*
Offenbach, Jacques, 239–40
opera, 55–59, 123–24, 125–28, 134–40, 148–51. *See also* music

patriarchy, 177–79
pederasty, 142
Perseus, 102–3
phallus, 26–29, 38–40, 61–64, 132–33 and *passim*
phantom (Nicolas Abraham), 128
piano, 172, 201–2
Pope, Alexander, 259–60
psychoanalysis, 8–9, 21–26, 262 and *passim*. *See also* Feminist psychoanalysis
Puccini, Giacomo, 123; *Madame Butterfly*, 125–28

race, 6–7, 127, 159–60, 183
Raglund-Sullivan, Ellie, 27
representation, 19, 180–83
"Rime of the Ancient Mariner, The" (Coleridge), 30–32, 72–73, 96
Rimsky-Korsakov, Nikolai, 238

Rosamunde (Schubert; dream), 4, 49, 191–92
Rosen, Charles, 45, 81
Russell, Jane, 174–76

Sacher-Masoch, Leopold von, 150
Sacks, Oliver, 155–56
Sacks, Peter, 74
de Sade, Donatien-Alphonse-François, 177
Sand, George, 234–25
Scheherazade (Rimsky-Korsakov), 238
Schreber, Daniel Paul, 164, 168
Schubert, Franz, 2. See also *Rosamunde*
Schumann, Robert, 4–5; Symphony No. 4, 239
screen dream, 49
Sedgwick, Eve Kosofsky, 197
seduction, primal, 153
semiotic, the, 53
Shakespeare, William, 66, 141, 209; *Coriolanus*, 142–43
Sibelius, Jean, Violin Concerto, 241
Silverman, Kaja, 23, 41, 121
Simpson, Nicole Brown, 18, 189, 194
Simpson, O. J., 18, 189
sirens, 173–76
sorcerer's apprentice, 61
Stevens, Wallace, 105
Strindberg, August, 101
superego, 23–26, 120, 158, 169, 203, 247, 258
symbolic order, 28, 42, 163, 214

Tales of Hoffmann (Offenbach), 239–40
Tennyson, Alfred Lord, 14, 15, 18, 20, 46, 60, 110 and *passim; In Me-*moriam, 14–15, 65–76, 87–88, 163–68, 198–99, 252–53; "The Lady of Shalott," 104; *The Princess*, 66–67, 210–12; "Recollection of the Arabian Nights," 50–54, 253–54; "Tithonus," 88–89
theft, and masculine identity, 253–55
The Thing, 42
thyrsis, 61–64
Tolstoy, Leo, 18, 20, 81, 82 and *passim; Anna Karenina*, 112; "The Kreutzer Sonata," 11–12, 30–33, 37, 44–45, 77–80, 95–96, 108, 114–19, 121, 133, 134–35, 140, 144, 171–72, 185–86, 194–96, 202, 208–9, 250
Tovey, Donald Francis, 82
transsexual wish, 164–68

Ulysses, 173–76

Verdi, Giuseppe, *Ernani*, 56–57; *Aida, La Traviata, Il Trovatore*, 137; *Otello*, 209
violin, 171, 238–42
virgule, 62

Wagner, Richard, 123, 137; *Tristan und Isolde*, 135, 140; *Parsifal*, 123–24
Wandering Jew, 32
Whitman, Walt, 14–15, 18, 19, 20, 46, 60, 90–91, 144, 199–200, 204–5 and *passim;* "As I Ebb'd with the Ocean of Life," 106, 250–52; "As If a Phantom Caress'd Me," 29; "As Once I Pass'd Through a Populous City," 99–100; "The City Dead House," 180–82; "I Sing the Body Elec-

tric," 14–15, 161–63, 226–27;
"Proud Music of the Storm,"
55–59, 110, 254; "The Sleepers," 91–94, 225, 227–28; "So
Long," 199–200; *Song of Myself*,
34–36, 106–7, 109, 148–51,
174, 254
Wilde, Oscar, 2
Winckelmann, Johann Joachim,
141
Winslow, Forbes, 65

wolf dreams: first, 47–49, 193; second, 85–86, 137–38, 144, 152,
184, 193, 264
Wolf Man, 18, 48, 152
Wordsworth, William, 75–76

Yonge, Mary (and William), 206–7

Žižek, Slavoj, 41–42
Zola, Émile, *La Bête humaine*, 243–
46; *Thérèse Raquin*, 181–82, 195

Compositor:	G&S Typesetters, Inc.
Music setter:	Mansfield Music Graphics, Inc.
Text:	10/15 Janson
Display:	Janson
Printer and binder:	Thomson-Shore, Inc.